**A COLLECTION OF KNOWLEDGE FROM
16 SUCCESSFUL RURAL BUSINESS WOMEN**

RURAL BUSINESS WOMEN

Inspiration and advice to grow your business from regional Australia

Curated by Sarah Walkerden

First published by Busybird Publishing 2021

Copyright © 2021 Individual authors

Paperback: 978-1-922691-25-5
Ebook: 978-1-922691-26-2

This work is copyright. Apart from any use permitted under the *Copyright Act 1968*, no part of this publication may be reproduced, stored in a retrieval system or transmitted in any form or by any means, electronic, mechanical, photocopying, recording or otherwise, without the prior written permission of Sarah Walkerden.

The information in this book is based on the author's experiences and opinions. The author and publisher disclaim responsibility for any adverse consequences, which may result from use of the information contained herein. Permission to use any external content has been sought by the author. Any breaches will be rectified in further editions of the book.

Cover Image: Sarah Walkerden

Cover design: Busybird Publishing

Layout and typesetting: Busybird Publishing

Busybird Publishing
2/118 Para Road
Montmorency, Victoria
Australia 3094
www.busybird.com.au

Contents

Introduction ... 1

PART 1 - Mindset

Chapter One
Believe to Achieve ... 7
By Janiece McCarthy

Chapter Two
My Journey of Self-Discovery – What Rock Was I Living Under? ... 29
By Jo Collier

Chapter Three
Overcoming Obstacles ... 43
By Linda Goldspink-Lord

Chapter Four
The Importance of Community and How to Find It ... 57
By Clare Doye

Chapter Five
Building Psychological Flexibility to Build Your Business and Thrive in Adversity ... 71
By Stephanie Schmidt

PART 2 - Getting Started

Chapter Six
How to Start an Online Business ... 97
By Sarah Britz

Chapter Seven
Finding the Gaps in the Market (And What Sets You Apart) ... 119
By Lisa Woods

Chapter Eight
The Value of Education for Women: An Opportunity to Poverty-Proof Your Future ... 131
By Gillian Hehir

Chapter Nine
Bootstrapping Your Business   143
By Anna Barwick

PART 3 - Marketing

Chapter Ten
Make Marketing a Priority in Your Business   157
By Jenn Donovan

Chapter Eleven
Copywriting Essentials for Rural Businesses   191
By Sarah Walkerden

Chapter Twelve
Insights From a Start-Up: My First Year in Business   211
By Phillipa Lawson

Chapter Thirteen
Digital Marketing Essentials for Rural Businesses   223
By Sarah Walkerden

PART 4 - Systems for Growth

Chapter Fourteen
Bookkeeping to Grow Your Business   239
By Emily Sinderberry

Chapter Fifteen
The Art of Delegation – Even When You Don't Want To   255
By Melanie Fitzgibbon

Chapter Sixteen
Recognising Opportunities and Making Conscious, Considered Decisions   265
By Tracey Browning

Chapter Seventeen
Keeping the Businesswoman Alive – Reinventing Yourself   279
By Susie Williams

Conclusion   293

Introduction

When I embarked on this project to help entrepreneurs, I had no clue where it would lead me. All I had was a vision of bringing together a group of rural women in business to produce a one-of-a-kind book, the first to feature rural women who are doing fabulous things in business. My hope was to inspire other rural women to pursue their own businesses too.

I had no idea whether I was going to find enough willing contributors. I had no idea whether it would work. I had no idea just how much it would consume me, or just how much time I would need to dedicate to it.

However, I did manage to find this group of amazing women and I'm ever so grateful they chose to come on this journey with me.

The results have been magic.

Every author in this book have lived through their unique journeys, both in life and business. No two stories are the same and every chapter contains absolute gold in terms of advice and inspiration.

Making the time to write more than 3,000 words might seem relatively easy at first, but it really isn't once you sit down and attempt to do it. Every one of us have faced inner turmoil in trying to put everything we've learnt into one tiny chapter.

There have been tears, computer crashes and disruptions due to Covid-19 lockdowns. Many authors are juggling home-schooling, businesses and other life and farm commitments.

So, hats off to these wonderful rural ladies.

Some of them help run large farming enterprises while juggling their own businesses, others have forged livelihoods from the middle of the bush. Some live in large regional towns, others in tiny rural communities.

There's a diversity here and yet a unique closeness, one that will hopefully inspire other rural women to chase their business dreams too. It's a dream that is incredibly possible to achieve with the right knowledge, mental outlook, support, and an absolute tonne of sheer grit and determination (as well as a semi-reliable internet connection!).

I hope this book will provide both knowledge and inspiration in an easily accessible form. Read it from cover to cover the first time and keep it handy. You never know when you might need the insights or encouragement from a chapter or two.

The Four Sections

The collection of chapters is divided into four sections – Mindset, Getting Started, Marketing and Systems for Growth – which will help you at just about every stage of your business journey.

Mindset always comes first for me. It took me a few years in business to learn just how important a heathy and progressive mindset really is.

Your business is, and always will be, a reflection of you, as well as your thoughts, beliefs, motives, history and goals.

What you believe in your mind is what you tend to receive. When you want to reach a certain level in business or grow things further, you must first see it and feel it as being possible within you. Plus, all your belief systems and the "stories" you tell yourself need to be unpacked, understood, resolved and then evolve to match the new levels of success you wish to achieve.

Introduction

This might sound a bit "woo woo" to many of us practical rural entrepreneurs, but there's a very good chance that if you feel stuck in your business, it's due to your mental and emotional state, conditioning and beliefs. Evolve your mindset and you'll remove a lot of the perceived roadblocks when running your business.

The second section is Getting Started. This section has been designed to assist any rural woman who has an idea or a very new business and needs that little bit of knowledge and support to get things moving and gain that initial traction on a budget. Even if you're beyond this early stage in business, there's a good chance you'll still learn some great tips.

Thirdly, we have Marketing. This is my favourite topic as I'm a copywriter and marketer. Marketing is the number one driver of business success and growth. Without it, no one will know who you are. Therefore, I recommend referring to these chapters often.

Finally, we have Systems for Growth. We have a wonderful chapter on bookkeeping and accounting, which is fundamental to ensuring that you have a handle of your business finances. Plus, we have advanced topics such as delegation, recognising opportunities and reinventing yourself as you grow. Don't underestimate the power of these aspects to help you move forward.

Lastly, remember this, you're always more powerful than you think.

As rural, regional and remote women, we are incredibly strong, resilient and determined. Sometimes it's easier to put our business ideas on the bench due to farm, family or community commitments. As women, we're the masters of self-sacrifice and putting everyone else's dreams, goals and needs first.

We also tend to doubt ourselves and seek out all the evidence as to why we *shouldn't* pursue what we want. Please don't keep finding all the reasons why you can't and shouldn't.

You can and you should.

At any given time, you can prioritise what you want out of life, even when it starts out with the tiniest baby steps imaginable. The trick is to just start.

If you have an idea for a business – or want to grow your small business into something much bigger – just try it out. Back yourself and give it a red hot go.

Life is a huge adventure. It doesn't need to be hard or limited in any way.

Building a business could give you and your family all the freedom, flexibility and fun you could ever possibly dream of. And why wouldn't you go after that?

I hope this book is the source of inspiration you need.

Sarah Walkerden
The Rural Copywriter & Curator of *Rural Business Women*

Part 1

Mindset

Chapter One
Believe to Achieve

By Janiece McCarthy
Janiece McCarthy Coaching

They say that operating a successful business is 20% mechanics and 80% mindset. If you understand the factors influencing your business, you can adjust your focus to better address its needs.

Imagine this: you are physically working but your mind is on other things. You might be worrying about not having the money to do things, that your partner or family are not supportive, or that you don't understand marketing enough to accomplish your goals.

Take a step back and look at what's causing you to have these limiting beliefs. You can spend all the time in the world developing a solid business strategy, but it won't matter if your mindset is not in the right place.

You want to develop the mindset of a champion. To do this, you must first allow yourself to let go of the thoughts that are preventing you from moving forward.

Imagine a marathon runner. They train, they believe that they will win the marathon.

Without belief in themselves, do you think they have a higher chance of winning or running further back in the pack?

Developing a Business Mindset

Building a great business takes more than passion, dedication and a strong work ethic. Entrepreneurs typically have a set of traits that set them apart from their competition. A solid concept may only get you so far, but the correct mindset can propel you through even the most difficult of challenges.

Your mindset is what you believe, your attitudes, and the way you think about your business and yourself, which goes a long way in determining the success of what you do. You can develop an entrepreneurial mindset to change the way you think fundamentally. Believe in your business and yourself!

The long-term success of your business depends on your ability to adapt. Find something you love doing and fight for it. One of the most important personality traits of any successful businessperson is determination.

It's not just about being able to withstand the challenges that confront you, or having a strong will and persistence, but also about being prepared. Planning your strategy is essential to you succeeding in your business.

Believe in Yourself and Your Business

Seven years ago, I left my full-time, well-paid teaching job to start a new portrait photography business.

I know, right? Who does that?

Because I had run a photography business prior to becoming a teacher, I expected smooth sailing through a calm sea, and I ventured into portrait photography domination! I believed that I would hit the ground running in my new business because I had a strong background as a professional photographer, and I taught photography and related subjects.

Well, I hate to admit it, but starting, managing and growing a successful business is a gazillion times harder than anyone expects. I should clarify that statement with: I expected everything to happen overnight. But, of course, it didn't.

And, because I wanted everything to happen quickly, I found myself working day and night, totally consumed like a crazy woman.

There are two insights that I'd like to share with you that got me through the start-up stage of building my business:

1. LOVE your business.

If you are doing something that you love, then that alone can help you ride through the fog and wild seas until you get to the point where you know you're sailing into bright skies and smooth waters.

There was nothing about the early days in business that seemed easy: purchasing new equipment was fun but setting up the tech side was pretty daunting. Making the studio look pretty was fun but getting my head around online advertising was a head-spin.

I took some time to do a short business course to fill the gaps in my knowledge, i.e. I had run a photography business pre-Facebook, so I upskilled to make my transition into the digital business world.

This is a continuing theme for me: I have an inquisitive mind and I like to know how things work. But one BIG thing that I learnt was that there are others who can do the things that I don't like doing or that takes a whole heap of time away from my core business of taking portraits, and learning to delegate is crucial.

2. Your business is an ONGOING challenge

As an entrepreneur (yes, that's you) it's not like there's a finish line. So, it's better to take a constant jog rather than a sprint so that you don't burn yourself out prematurely.

I spent my first couple of years working in the studio through the day and staying up editing at home half the night. I cranked out Facebook and Instagram content continuously because I thought that's what I had to do. I physically could not do any more portraits that I was doing because all the other work was holding me back.

To grow my business and prevent burnout, I realised that I had to employ skilled people to do the things that I didn't enjoy or have time for, so that I could spend more time doing the things that I enjoyed, including time with my family! I hired a retoucher, a person to handle my social media, and an office manager to handle the accounts and client management.

It seemed like a gamble (I should say educated gamble) at the time, but I did my figures and it paid off within a matter of weeks. I doubled my turnover in the next twelve months, exceeding my predictions.

As the business grew, it needed me in different ways. The team and I developed processes and procedures that we documented so that in the event of staff leaving, new staff could be inducted easily.

Businesses that run well have systems in place. Look at McDonald's: a prime example of everyone understanding their defined role and knowing how to carry it out.

Develop a Growth Mindset

First, let's look at a *Fixed Mindset.* This is the belief that our qualities (talent or intelligence) are fixed traits that we can't change. People with this mindset believe that talent alone leads to success.

On the other hand, a *Growth Mindset* is believing that our intelligence can grow with time and experience. This mindset encourages us to put in extra time and effort, which leads to higher achievement. Everything we read, study and experience can lead to better understandings, greater knowledge and higher achievement.

A *Fixed Mindset* limits our capacity for learning, whereas a *Growth Mindset* helps us reach our full potential. This is a simplified look at mindsets, but you get the general idea.

I find the study of psychology fascinating. There are many other types of mindsets that are worth looking at: *Fear versus Fearless* – seeing life through a lens of fear can be intimidating; *Reactive versus Proactive* – proactive people don't let circumstances control them, wasting their energy or time, they focus on what they can manage.

Success and happiness are all about mindset. What you think, you become. Your mindset doesn't just affect how you see the world. It shapes your responses and actions even if you don't realise it. Developing the right mindset is crucial to succeeding in anything.

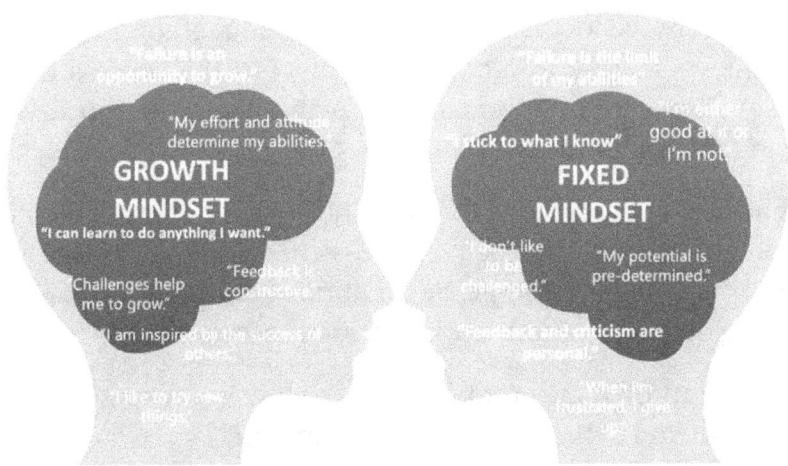

A Growth Mindset helps us reach our full potential.

Find Your Vision, Mission and Passion

What's your life purpose? Find your *why*.

Having a clear vision of why you do what you do gives you direction and guides you in making important business and life decisions.

In the planning stages of my portrait business, I thought long and hard about my *why* because, by doing that, every piece of my marketing would relate to my underlying reason for doing what I do.

My belief, as a specialist women's portrait photographer, was that women generally don't like (or even *hate*) photos of themselves. It was my *mission* to change the way women see themselves through creating beautiful portraits that they love and that their families will treasure for many years to come. This underpinned all my marketing messages and helped me build a very successful portrait studio.

My *passion* was to help women feel beautiful and to see themselves, sometimes for the first time, as beautiful.

By tying my vision, mission and passion together, I was able to achieve success in monetary terms, but the success that I achieved personally seemed far greater, even though it was intangible and unmeasurable.

What does success mean to you? There's a difference between achieving success and being successful. Achieving success is about reaching a specific destination. Being successful is a state of mind. It's about appreciating the journey.

Create your own measure of success. How will you get there? How will you achieve your mission in life?

Give Yourself Permission

Give yourself permission to succeed. What if the only thing holding you back from experiencing the life you want and building the business of your dreams is yourself?

In general, women tend to struggle with a wider confidence gap than men. When you own a business, you can only advance it to a level that your mind perceives is possible. Once you expand your view of what is possible, you need to give yourself permission and believe that you can reach your goals.

Build a business that is consistent with who you are as a person. I was never comfortable with sharing my personal life all over my social media even though I respect those who choose to do so. I'm far from the stereotypical photographer and, while service-based, my entrepreneurial spirit saw my business evolve over time.

On reflection, I realise that my ten-plus years as a teacher was, in essence, about helping others, helping teens and young adults do well at school and enjoy their lives.

I lead an amazing team of twenty-two teaching staff to energise and support them in their teaching journey. My photography business aimed at empowering women and provided an opportunity for me to support local charities as well.

In a continuously evolving career, I am combining my education background with my business experience to help photographers learn about the business side of photography and providing online courses to help them to achieve their goals.

Truthfully, just because a direction was right for you in the beginning doesn't mean that you need to stay rigid by doing the same thing now. It's natural to evolve and change over time. You may develop a new service or product, and you'll find that most businesses need to do that to thrive in changing markets.

Give yourself permission to be happy. Find the people to work with and business opportunities that make you excited so you are left feeling satisfied and fulfilled at the end of each day.

Overcoming Imposter Syndrome

Many high achievers are victims of imposter syndrome at some stage in their career. Deep down they feel like complete frauds, with the thought that their accomplishments are the result of unanticipated luck.

The psychological phenomenon, known as *imposter syndrome*, reflects a belief that you're inadequate and unqualified despite evidence indicating that you're skilled and quite successful.

It's generally accompanied and intensified by perfectionism, black-and-white thinking and an intense fear of rejection and failure. These thought patterns create a perfect storm of insecurity, anxiety and stress.

Causes of imposter syndrome can be:

- **Social Conditioning:** Women are continually examining themselves for flaws and fretting over whether they measure up.

- **Family Conditioning:** You could have been predisposed to imposter syndrome if you come from a family with high standards or if your parents were dismissive of you.

- **Critical Self-Talk:** You're more likely to feel like you're not good enough and don't belong if you believe any of your negative thoughts about yourself.

Dr. Valerie Young is an expert in this field and categorises *Imposter Syndrome* into subgroups: the Perfectionist, the Superwoman/man, the Natural Genius, the Soloist and the Expert.[1]

- **The Perfectionist:** Perfectionism and imposter syndrome often go hand in hand. Perfectionists set unrealistically high expectations for themselves, and when they don't meet those expectations, they are filled with self-doubt and anxiety over not measuring up.

  Perfectionists have trouble delegating and may also be control freaks, believing that they must do everything themselves if they want something done right.

- **The Superwoman:** Do you stay at the office beyond the point of what's necessary for a day's work? Do you get stressed when you're not working and find downtime completely wasteful? Have you neglected to prioritise family gatherings or things that you enjoy because you believe that relaxing is a waste of time that could be better spent working?

  Imposter syndrome takes on the guise of a workaholic, being addicted to the validation that comes from working.

- **The Natural Genius:** Like perfectionists, these types of imposters set their internal bar impossibly high, judging themselves not just on unreasonable aspirations, but also on their ability to get everything right the first time.

  The Natural Genius was always the smart one as a child, consistently getting excellent marks,

---

1 - Young, Dr Valerie, The Secret Thoughts of Successful Women: Why Capable People Suffer from the Impostor Syndrome and How to Thrive in Spite of It, New York, Crowne Publishing Group, 2011

excelling without much effort. When they are faced with a setback, their confidence is bruised and they often avoid challenges because they don't want the embarrassment.

- The Soloist: It's okay to be independent but not at your own expense. Soloists are unable to accept support from others, believing that doing so exposes their phoniness.

- The Expert: Experts assess their abilities based on "what" they know and "how much" they can do. They are afraid of being exposed as inexperienced or unknowledgeable because they believe that they will never know enough. They are constantly pursuing training or qualifications because they believe that to succeed, they must further develop their skills.

While upskilling and keeping ahead of the competition is beneficial, the constant search for new knowledge can be a form of procrastination.

IMPOSTER SYNDROME

What my brain tells me.....

... but in reality

Other peoples Knowledge & skills

My own Knowledge & skills

Other peoples Knowledge & skills

My own Knowledge & skills

Reframe the way you think about your achievements.

The study of psychology and *Imposter Syndrome* can be enlightening, but no matter what *imposter traits* you may identify with, if you struggle with confidence, you are not alone. Studies suggest that 70% of people experience imposter syndrome at some stage in their career.[2]

Relax! You know your stuff. Sure, you might not know *every single thing*, but you know enough to not doubt yourself. One thing my dear dad said to me many years ago is that you learn your whole life.

The fact that you are reading this book indicates that you take your journey as an entrepreneur seriously. The wisdom that you glean from these pages will have a compounding effect on the way you think and perceive yourself and your business.

As a teacher I would ask my students to do a quick online quiz to determine what kind of learner they were, i.e. visual, auditory, reading/writing or kinaesthetic. Similarly, studying a little psychology and discovering what makes you tick can be enlightening. It can help you understand not only the thought processes of others, but also of yourself.

Achieve Your Goals and Dreams

I was listening to Mick Molloy's drive time show on the radio when I was driving home, and he said something that made me laugh out loud:

"You can't fly like an eagle when you're surrounded by turkeys."

A comical quote that made me think of this part of the chapter that I have been formulating over past weeks.

---

[2] - Sakulku, J. & Alexander, J. (2011). The imposter phenomenon. International Journal of Behavioral Science, 6(1), 73-92

I also sourced this original quote by Gary Kent, one of Hyde School's (USA) all-time great teachers and coaches:

> *"You can't soar like an eagle with the mindset of a turkey.*
>
> *If you don't believe you can fly, you will never fly.*
>
> *If you don't believe you are capable of soaring to the top of your own mountain peak in life, you will never try and therefore never succeed.*

If your mind is full of negativity … you will never see the positive.

> *If your mind is full of limitations, it is closed off to opportunities and possibilities that might be right in front of your face."*

Keep this in mind. I'll come back to this later.

Develop Routines and Processes

Putting some structure into your day may be the best thing that you can do for yourself and your business.

As a woman, I'm meant to be a multitasker, managing multiple tasks at the same time, but what I have discovered about myself is that I work best when I can give my total concentration to *one big thing* at a time, without a heap of interruptions or things to take me away from my main goal.

Take writing this chapter for example. I knew that I would need several blocks of time to systematically complete each section.

So, I divided the task up into smaller sections and used my calendar to block out time for each section. I added a bit of contingency time as well and *voilà*! Chapter complete (well, almost, because I'm still writing this bit …).

I would strongly recommend developing a routine to keep you on track. Here's a starting point for keeping yourself organised throughout your week:

1. Write down all the tasks you need to do on a daily basis. You'll be surprised by how many things you identify!

2. Make another list, divided into days of the week, including Saturday and Sunday.

3. Block out your family time … yep, first thing before everything else, because if you don't, you'll be the worst person in the world for letting work encroach on the time you could be spending with your family and friends. Work (and this is the truth) is NOT more important than your family and friends. Also, block out time for exercise.

4. Enter your wake-up time and your bedtime. Everything else will have to fit in between these times.

5. Block out time for the major must-do tasks of each day. Schedule time for opening and responding to emails. Don't be tempted to take a sneak peek at emails (or socials) when you should be concentrating on another task. It's a sure way of taking yourself off on a tangent. Set an autoresponder on your emails gently outlining to your clients the times that you will respond to emails.

6. Once you have all your tasks identified and scheduled on your calendar, trial it to see if it works in practice. Tweak it if you need to for the second week and then try to stick with it for twenty-one days. This is the 21/90 rule and is a popular method to build good habits. Simply commit to a goal for twenty-one consecutive days, and after three weeks, the pursuit of that goal should have become a habit. Once you've established that habit, you continue to do it for another ninety days to lock it in.

There are a number of processes that are absolutely essential to efficiently run any kind of business, regardless of size, industry or location. These are processes that, without clear documentation and management, may cause hold-ups that stifle growth or, at worst, force a business to close its doors.

You can develop templates to guide you through your processes with consistent results. Here are a few:

- Client onboarding workflow, checklist, email sequence, welcome packet
- Workflow for blog posts/social media
- Telephone scripts
- Product development
- Sales/presentation process, creating invoices and payment processes
- Ordering process
- Procurement: supplier evaluation, purchasing, selecting vendors, establishing payment processes

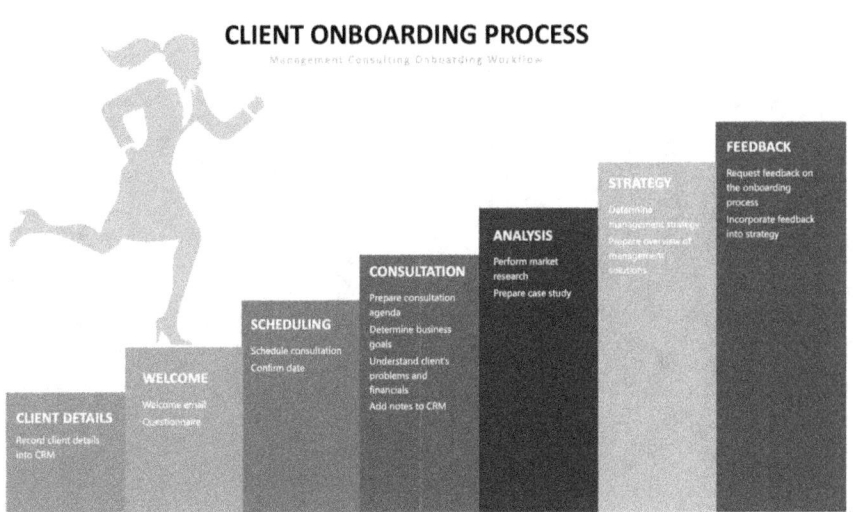

Client onboarding process.

Set Your Goals

If you want to succeed, you need to set goals. Without goals you lack focus and direction. Setting goals not only helps you to change your life's path, but it also gives you a benchmark for measuring whether you have actually succeeded.

Every successful business has clear, set and articulated goals to attain specific objectives. Set goals for yourself that motivate you. Get your staff onboard by getting them involved in the goal-setting process.

When setting a goal, make sure it is motivational. Write down *why* it is important to you. Ask yourself, "If I were to share my goal with others, how would I explain it to them?" Write it out and pin it to your noticeboard to keep you motivated and on track.

Set SMART goals. SMART is an acronym for: Specific, Measurable, Attainable, Relevant and Time-Based objectives.

SMART GOALS

SPECIFIC	MEASURABLE	ACHIEVABLE	RELEVANT	TIME-BOUND
• What do I want to achieve? • Why do I want to accomplish this? • Who needs to be involved to accomplish this goal? • What are the requirements? • What are the constraints?	• How will I measure my progress? • How will I know when the goal is achieved?	• How can the goal be accomplished? • Do I have the necessary resources and skills to achieve this goal? • If not, how can I build my skills? • What are the logical steps I should take?	• Is this the right time? • Why should I achieve this goal? • Is this goal in line with my life long objectives?	• How long will it take to accomplish this goal? • When is the completion of this goal due? • When am I going to work on this goal?

Set clear SMART goals for your business.

- **Set Specific Goals:** Be clear on what your goals are. Your objectives must be precise and well defined. Keep in mind that your goals need to guide your business.

- **Set Measurable Goals:** Include specific numbers, dates and other details in your goals so that you can track your progress. Otherwise, you won't know when you've achieved your goal. Rather than a goal to "lower expenses", be specific. For example, "reduce expenses by 2% in thirty days and 5% in twelve months." You need to have a way of measuring your success.

- **Set Attainable Goals:** Make sure you'll be able to achieve your objectives. You will erode your confidence if you set a goal that you have little chance of attaining. However, resist the temptation to set goals that are too easy. By setting realistic goals, with an element of challenge, your success will give you great satisfaction.

- **Set Relevant Goals:** Align your goals with the direction you want to take your business.

- **Set Time-Bound Goals:** Set a deadline for each goal that you set. By setting a deadline, it creates a sense of urgency and prevents you from letting time slip away from you. Create an Action Plan of steps to get you to achieve each goal. Crossing them off as you go can give you a sense that you are making progress as you get closer to your goal.

- **Set Goals in Writing:** Use a SMART goals template to physically write down each of your goals. By doing this, it makes your goals real and tangible.

Learning From Your Wins and Fails

You know the old saying, "If at first you don't succeed, try, try again." But in our *success-obsessed society*, is it okay to fail?

Even the most successful entrepreneurs have experienced failures or rejection. Everyone needs to undergo mistakes to enable themselves to grow. However, the depth or impact of a failure can be mitigated by working on your business mindset and planning to succeed.

Projecting a long-term vision for your business or project, evolving along the way to meet buyer demand, sharing your vision with employees to get them on board, are practices that work well to promote wins.

One main strategy to build into your plan to have greater wins is to understand who your ideal client is.

Win more clients by understanding *who* they are. There's a reason why it's highly suggested that you build your client *avatar*. Your ideal client is the one who gets their exact needs met by your product or service. You can better understand your ideal client by understanding:

- Who they are (their goals, values, demographics, etc)
- Where they are hanging out online and offline
- What challenges (or pain points) they have

Understanding your ideal client will help you to know what content marketing to use (blog posts, lead magnets, videos, podcasts), which platforms to use (Facebook, Instagram, Twitter, LinkedIn), and what content for copywriting and email marketing to use to get better open rates for your campaigns.

Surround Yourself with Like-Minded People

Remember the saying, "Don't surround yourself with turkeys"? To "soar like an eagle" you need to release yourself from what is holding you back, metaphorically speaking.

Let me explain.

I have been super lucky to have a supportive husband and family to encourage me in my entrepreneurial pursuits, but it hasn't always been that way. And I remember too well the struggle, self-doubt and heartache that went along with establishing my first business all those years ago.

I was surrounded by good friends, but they didn't share my vision. They were content in their world and, I suppose, didn't see any need to look beyond it. But I did. I had a dream very early on, and it meant releasing myself from limitations. Don't get me wrong. I'm still friends with many of them, but I also sought out others who thought the same way I did.

When I went to university as a mature-age student, I was the first one in my social group to do so. I remember having to deflect a lot of criticism at the time, but I was determined to follow my dream.

When I opened my first photographic studio, I had arrived in the business community.

Here's a tip. Photography was my skill, but I was a businesswoman. Making that distinction can make a world of difference in the way you think about your business.

Surround yourself with like-minded people. They will share similar opinions, ideas and interests. Get to know local women in business. Chatting with them about business can benefit both of you. Join your local Chamber of Commerce.

Join businesswomen's groups. They often meet socially each month. If there's not a businesswomen's group in your area, start one!

Be Open to Finding a Mentor

Now, I'm not just saying that because I am a mentor. I believe in life-long education and always have my head in a textbook or listening to a business podcast. I have worked with several mentors over the years.

Highly effective mentors care about the next generation's success and the positive reputation of the industry. They share experiences rather than advise, are comfortable to talk to, and they provide quality feedback.

I'm a firm believer in finding a mentor in the industry in which you work. Photography businesses are idiosyncratic or distinctive in that they are selling an experience and a product, both of which are intangible at the outset. The photographer is basically promising that they will deliver. The photography industry is highly speculative, and marketing must be highly emotive.

There's no right or wrong time to work with a mentor. You could develop an ongoing relationship, or your connection could be project specific. Your mentor (or business coach) will become your confidant, friend and cheerleader! They can help you navigate a pathway for your business and reach your goals quicker than going at it alone.

Conclusion

There is a lot to consider when starting and operating your own business, but the fact that you are reading this book of aspiring entrepreneurs proves that you have what it takes.

Self-education and opening your horizons are ongoing throughout the life of an entrepreneur.

Develop a growth mindset. Love what you do and remind yourself why you are doing it. Set your goals. Write them on your noticeboard so you can read them every day.

Use a calendar to keep yourself on track while allowing yourself some downtime to recharge. Surround yourself with people who will support you in your journey.

Believe in yourself. You can do this!

About the Author

As CEO of an award-winning photographic studio, Artisan House of Photography, Janiece McCarthy built a highly successful 6-figure business from the ground up. First established in 2000 the studio began as a wedding and family portrait studio and went on to specialise in Women's Portraiture, Personal Branding and Boudoir Photography.

Janiece is author of the coffee table book and Amazon best-seller *50 Fabulous Women: Every Woman Has A Story* a collection of photographs and stories from women who have overcome some of life's biggest challenges, revealing their resilience and great courage.

Janiece has a Bachelor of Arts Degree (Photography & Art History), Cert IV in Business Management, and is a postgraduate qualified education professional with over 10 years experience as a qualified teacher, trainer, curriculum developer and educational leader.

In 2020 Janiece established her online education business JanieceMcCarthy.com for professional photographers to gain valuable business skills and help them to increase their bookings, maximise sales and create marketing opportunities.

Enjoying a successful career as a professional photographer, Janiece combines her business acumen, education background, and her passion to share knowledge, with photographers to help them build the photography business of their dreams!

Chapter Two
My Journey of Self-Discovery –
What Rock Was I Living Under?

By Jo Collier
My People Group/My Mentor 4 Recruiters

During the first Covid-19 lockdown in 2020 where we spent about six weeks at home, I wondered, what is happening to us, how will this end, will we go into a great depression, when will my business get any clients trading again?

I believed that I needed a personal coach. I cannot tell you why, but the universe was pulling me in that direction. I also knew that I wanted a non-traditional coach, someone not vanilla, someone out of the box.

I had been watching Nic Stewart's posts on Facebook and thought why not, she seemed raw and interesting, and I knew I wanted someone to help me learn about myself that was not from a corporate.

I had met Nic a few years earlier and we had undertaken a session for me. It was quite insightful, and I remember one powerful point where we discussed my creation of an income that was ideally not to be linked to time.

We agreed on a weekly session for ten weeks via Zoom. I can clearly remember the first session as if it was yesterday. She explained to me in a very functional way that I came from a very strong masculine energy level. I was strong, driven, focused, powerful, decisive, resilient and goal oriented.

I would make full use of the day and I was fast talking, fast breathing and fast walking. I came from a place of thinking, planning, problem solving and logical. I was very resilient.

Yes, that was me – and I was proud of this. These were the traits that helped me rise to the top of the corporate recruitment world – to be the CEO of a very large recruitment firm. To be known and respected as a high achiever, this masculine energy had served me well.

But I was curious. Nic spoke about the feminine energy – the soft, intuitive, nurturing and compassionate energy. The slow speaking, slow breathing and present energy. The vulnerable, sensual and feeling energy.

I wanted to know more, so I researched on how to understand and develop the feminine energy.

Discovering and Developing My Feminine Energy

First, I had to *slow down* – breathe slow, walk slow, talk slow and eat slow. In terms of breathing slow and deep into my body, this was hard and I was not good at it. I had to breathe deeper and slower, and let it out with a noise. I could not make a sound, and I didn't understand why. But when Nic demonstrated the masculine energy breathing, I could make that happen so easily.

This was an interesting experience given that I would usually wake up, drink coffee and think of all the things I needed to do for the day. I would feed my horses while thinking about my to-do list and what I will do first. I ate my breakfast, not even sure if I ever thought about how the food tasted, let alone devour with pleasure. And by the time I started on my to-do list, I was already exhausted by my frantic pace of doing everything.

So, I slowed down. I fed my horses while being present – I enjoyed the company of the horses and the outdoors and did not allow my to-do list to overtake my thoughts. I drank and tasted my morning coffee and felt the effects. I had my breakfast without tapping on my laptop and then slowly prioritised my first few tasks, doing them at an easy, slow pace.

It was effective. In fact, I was so much more effective and much more thorough.

> *"You can be vulnerable and still be powerful. You can have a gentle heart but still be rock solid at the core. You can be as calm as a breeze but as fierce as a tiger, the best people embody both sides."*
>
> *– Matthew Hussey*

I wanted to learn more, so I delved further and learnt about some actions to take to enhance the feminine energy.

1. Use Your Intuition

Practice using your intuition and trusting it, instead of overthinking and using your logical mind. When you need to make a decision, let it come from your gut. Intuition is a feminine superpower.

2. Create Spaciousness

This is about saying no to things and doing less, taking things off the to-do list instead of adding them on, and actually letting there be spaciousness in your calendar instead of every week being crammed. The feminine energy is less about doing and more about being.

3. Connecting with the Body

The feminine energy is about connection to the body, so check in with your body every day, talk to your body, and touch your body. Take up dance classes, start yoga, or just dance for five minutes every day in front of the mirror.

4. Activate Your Pleasure and Sensuality

Bring more pleasure into your daily life. Think about what brings you pleasure. Is it dancing, music, food, wine, sex or massage? The feminine energy loves all pleasures. When do you feel sexiest and most sensual? Do something that helps you feel sexy every day and allow yourself to really enjoy life's pleasures without feeling guilty.

Why Does the World Encourage and Celebrate Masculine Energy?

I believe that masculine energy is more widely accepted because we see feminine energy as soft, weak and vulnerable, which does not fit with the economic-driven world. In business, we love goals, structure, outcomes and dominance.

Companies generally do not value compassionate, nurturing or intuitive traits, even though these elements bring out the best in people.

In my corporate career, we celebrated growth, profit and outdoing the competitors. My remuneration plan was completely linked to those factors. We become conditioned to this reality and before you know it, this is how we survive.

I was the gold medallist for being resilient, but I was sad at how many relationships in business I had missed because I never nurtured them. How many people did I work with that I did not truly get to know?

I feel that my generation was on the cusp of the rise of the masculine energy – we wanted careers and equal opportunities, and so we consciously or sub-consciously embodied masculine energy to get ahead.

I developed a great corporate business acumen language and could say what the relevant stakeholders wanted to hear. I wore mostly black pant suits, and although I never succumbed to playing golf as a network and business opportunity, I bet plenty of others have.

Seven Archetypes of Feminine Energy

When I was going through the coaching with Nic, I realised that I could hardly remember the decade or so from my early thirties to my mid-forties where I retired from corporate life. Furthermore, I took this masculine energy into my own business – I did not know any different.

Here I was with my own business, operating like a mouse in wheel – go, go, go, and stop and sleep, and go, go, go, and stop and sleep. Where was the fun, where was the pleasure, where was the adventure, where was the real relationships?

I now developed a thirst for wanting to learn more about feminine energy as I knew so deeply this was my Achilles heel and I wanted it to be my strength.

I delved further to learn about Carl Jung's seven archetypes of feminine energy – the Mother, the Maiden, the Lover, the Huntress, the Wild Woman, the Wise Woman and the Queen.

The Mother

The Mother represents the nurturer, the lover and the caretaker. You embody the Mother by attuning yourself with nature and Mother Earth, mindfully slowing down, simplify and minimise your life, curate rituals and be creative with your hands.

The shadow side of the Mother is where you as a person gives too much, often neglecting yourself and your own needs. You need to be able to identify this, step away and invest in your self-care, because you are worth it.

The Maiden

The Maiden represents innocence, playfulness, enthusiasm and readiness to take on the world. You embody the Maiden by being enthusiastic, youthful and vivacious. The Maiden does not want to sit around and relax, she is creative and assertive, and it is a great energy to tap into for some fun.

The shadow side of the Maiden can be naïve, a people pleaser and someone who tends to mould herself into what others want her to be. She can be co-dependent and, as a result, is easily drawn into unhealthy relationships.

The Queen

The Queen is the boss of her life and her power, and above all, knows her worth. She is constantly up-levelling and laser-focused on her journey. You can embody the Queen by investing in your own growth and make those big decisions that you have feared so far in your life. Everything you desire is on the other side of fear, so take charge of the situation and believe that you have got this and is worthy.

The shadow side of the Queen is that with great power comes great responsibility, so the Queen needs to be conscious not to take advantage of that strength. She needs to be aware of boundaries and can still feel easily threatened by other women.

The Huntress

The Huntress is drawn by her fierce focus and is goal oriented, using her independence and courage to lead the way. Above all else, she desires freedom and will stand up for herself and value every opportunity to get there.

You embody the Huntress by acknowledging that it is time to pack your bras and go on an adventure to mindfully hunt for that which you want the most. Sharpen up your skillset or simply go hard in your next workout. This archetype encourages you to be a goal getter.

The shadow side of the Huntress is that she is very proud, independent and therefore is not always fully open to vulnerability or intimacy and can struggle with relationships.

The Lover

The Lover has a magnetic feeling towards having more love and passion in their life, but she is also creatively charged with a deep desire to connect with others. The deeper she comes into self-love, the healthier the love she attracts.

To embody the Lover, you need to take the opportunity to indulge in self-pleasure, massage, feast on delicious foods, express yourself through dance and wear clothes that make you feel most divine.

The shadow side of the Lover is that while she may welcome in the energy of desire, she can also take on the role of temptress or seductress, using her sexuality to manipulate, break hearts along the way and find herself in unwanted drama.

The Wild Woman

The Wild Woman is the one who strives for freedom in all aspects of her life. She desires the ability to tap into her mystical magic and awaken her inner enchantress. She has an awakened soul and connects deeply to herself and her spirit.

To embody the Wild Woman, spend some time alone with your thoughts as this enables you to be more connected to your intuition. Reduce stimulating activities and spend time in the wilderness, practise fierce embodiment and be sure to speak your truth with conviction and certainty.

The shadow side of the Wild Woman can be dangerous, unpredictable and chaotic. She needs to find ways to express anger in a healthy way.

The Wise Woman

The Wise Woman embraces how in-tune she is to her intuition and allows herself to come into her own power. She is a teacher who knows her own power and expresses herself with peace, strength and sincerity. She has met her shadow-self many times and knows how to consciously work with her rather than resist her.

To embody the Wise Woman, you need to journal, journal, journal, and use this time to ask the universe to speak through you and call in new signs from spiritual energies to help guide you in the right direction.

The shadow of the Wise Woman may feel lonely at times, as though there is no place in society for her. You will notice your introverted self go against you if you are struggling to express yourself emotionally.

Understanding My Archetypes

I operate easily as the Huntress, the Wise Woman, the Queen and to my surprise the Mother. Although, I am not an actual mother, I have a fur family that I am dedicated to. I am not very good at self-care and feel guilty when I take time for myself.

The archetype I wish to develop is the Lover. I am an introvert and therefore I am so happy to spend large amounts of time by myself. My business is in people – recruitment and training – so I often feel depleted in energy as I give so much to others. I need to recharge by spending time by myself when I have my down time.

During the coaching process, I was presented with the concept of my shadow. Again, I was confused. But it was fascinating to learn that we all have shadows. We need to be aware of what is hidden and gradually heal those aspects of ourselves.

When I started on my shadow work, I often felt the way I felt as a child when I was forced to suppress my emotions. As I continued to explore and overcome these uncomfortable feelings, my eyes were opened to a whole new side of me that I had no idea existed.

Take the Huntress, which is my dominant feminine archetype in the shadow that I am very proud of. She is way too independent and not always fully open to vulnerability or intimacy, and she struggles with relationships.

Or take the shadow of the Wise Woman. This is representative of me, where my introversion works against me, and I can feel lonely at times and certainly not fit into generic society.

> *"We fear losing control by being in our feminine, but we actually GAIN more power, it comes from a more empowered place."*
>
> *– Regina Thomashauer*

Intentions and the Universe – Law of Attraction

The coaching with Nic introduced me to the Law of Attraction. Building a vision of what I want from life, I asked myself, what are my dreams and intentions? Now, this really intrigued me as I have always been a person that believes that you can do what you want. I am the kid from The Mallee that became a CEO of a large global corporate because I wanted it.

I urged the possibility to come to me and I took action. At thirty-six years old, I was appointed as CEO, and in my first year I delivered a profit improvement of 220% compared with the previous year.

I enrolled in a three-week manifesting program, which introduced many ways to manifest dreams and desires. I set my ten intentions, and since then I have worked on this every day. I know what it feels like as it is as if my dreams are here now.

I know what I want and why. I can see it, touch it, feel it and hear it. It makes me feel free with ease and flow, purpose and prosperity, no guilt.

When I delved into the intentions and life dreams, I used a framework around the following types:

- **Purpose/Calling:** Discover your true "genius" so that you can create a business or career that will allow you to share your gifts in your sweet spot and fulfill your life's mission.

- **Confidence:** Liberate yourself from the self-doubt and insecurity, become authentically confident and visible, and be recognised and rewarded for your contributions.

- **Love and Relationships:** Attract a true equal or transform your present relationship to become the intimate and loving relationship you yearn for.

- **Prosperity:** Make a shift from simply surviving to thriving financially.

- **Creativity:** Manifest your desires for more self-expression, fun and play, infusing your creativity into every aspect of your life.

- **Spirituality:** Become more spiritually connected and attuned to your own inner compass.

- **Health:** Have limitless energy once you break free from underlying barriers contributing to chronic health challenges such as depression and anxiety, lack of energy or feeling out of alignment, so that you can move forward with the work you are here to do.

- **Influence:** Contribute gifts and talents to empower others in your family, your community and the world at large.

I have taken on two types of intention – purpose and prosperity.

Through this process I have developed a new business, MyMentor 4 Recruiters, where I am developing and sharing the gems that I have learnt from more than thirty years in the industry.

My greatest achievements in my corporate career were from seeing others in the company and beyond progress in their career – become leaders, owners and excelling at their craft.

I have started my first program and gained some great energy and drive from sharing my secret sauce and seeing people grow.

My second intention was prosperity. Through this process I have learnt that I have a money mindset that is not progressive. I have always earned my money by working very hard, long hours. I did not feel that I deserved the money unless I worked into my personal hours.

I have learnt that money is an energy, not a bad energy. It provides opportunity and choices. The intention I set was to build a successful business, and coming into 2021, my recruitment company has doubled in revenue and the number of team members.

Power of Gratitude

Perhaps the big game changer for me more than anything else is the practice of simple gratitude. I was gifted *The Magic* by Rhonda Byrne, and I underwent the 28-day Gratitude practice. I discovered the power of thinking about and journaling your gratitude when you are feeling negative or overwhelmed.

As Byrne said, "No matter who you are, no matter where you are, no matter what your current circumstances, the magic of gratitude will change your entire life!"

My morning ritual starts with writing down what I am grateful for. It is such a great way for me to start the day, remind myself of all the great things that is happening for me and around me. I encourage everyone to consider this practise as it takes nothing more than a few minutes, a pen and paper, but the magic is in how powerful it makes you feel.

Where Am I Now?

I am on a journey for the rest of my life to learn more about myself. Why do I react in certain ways? Why do I feel so alive when I think of this? What triggers me into anger?

This has led to a new business, My Mentor 4 Recruiters, where I see it as my purpose to help others, in particular women in recruitment, discover themselves, understand themselves and continue to work on themselves to live life by design.

I feel that I was trapped and rewarded for living under a huge rock where I had no idea that there could be another way. A better way where I truly love my life each day.

I feel that there is now more than ever an opportunity to work towards an equilibrium of both masculine and feminine energies in the world and have an impact on people, companies and society in general.

In my mentorship business, I have incorporated developing my client's awareness of feminine and masculine energies, discovering which archetypes are their strength, which they need to work on and how, working on their intentions and dreams, and ensuring that they come from a place of gratitude daily.

I am so grateful that the universe brought my coach to me, that I have a passion to learn and that I now love my morning coffee where I sit and smell the wonders of the world and give thanks to all the amazing things, people, adventures, opportunities, purpose and prosperity in my life.

Life is for living fully not in parts, and I have always said, "Life is not a dress rehearsal, this is it." So, Let's Live It.

About the Author

Jo Collier – for 33 years I have worked in the recruitment industry where I have undertaken every role from permanent recruiting to National Sales, to CEO of Adecco to CEO of PeopleCo, a start-up.

Today, I have my own recruitment company – My People Group where we provide permanent recruitment services to family-owned entrepreneurial companies.

I have recently commenced a new company My Mentor 4 Recruiters where I coach and train recruiters on all the secret sauce I have learnt including my recent self-discovery.

Chapter Three
Overcoming Obstacles

By Linda Goldspink-Lord
Poseidon Animal Health

Calm Before the Storm

The thing about life is we never know what the next step will bring.

We set for ourselves goals and create plans. We dream of a future that perhaps we had imagined as a young person or a future that just allows you to be the person you always knew you would be. Our future planning doesn't usually take into consideration obstacles or challenges that might get in the way.

I've always been a person that likes to plan ahead, consider the big picture and then work out the best way to get there. I have vivid memories of myself as a young girl lying in bed and thinking about my life ahead.

I would wonder who my husband would be and how many children I would have. I always pictured horses in lush green paddocks, with a big country farmhouse in some country town, and I had very clear career ambitions. I wanted to be a vet and I dreamed of writing a book.

I remember taking veterinary medicine books out of the library as a ten-year-old and trying to summarise the anatomy of dogs and horses. An early birthday present was a red typewriter, and I would type chapter after chapter of my latest book, which always had the same theme. It was about a young girl who moved to the country and rescued horses and went on to win an Olympic medal in a horse event.

My love of animals and writing has never left me and in fact has helped me through some of the toughest challenges of my life.

In my daydreams of the future, I never imagined the challenges that life would throw at me, nor would I have wanted to.

We can make plans and we can have dreams and goals, but the amazing thing about life is that it has its own twists and turns, and the road to your ultimate goal has exits and detours you could never imagine or anticipate.

These obstacles can appear from nowhere and leave you breathless, at times rudderless and seemingly without the wind in your sails to guide you to a safer destination. Sometimes they can creep up on you and take you by surprise.

I remember so clearly my fortieth birthday in 2007.

Turning forty was a big deal for me. It was a milestone birthday and I had decided to have this great big party at our home with all the people in my life that were important to me.

Leading up to this event, I had begun to experience some minor health challenges, the ones that you can always blame on something else. Headaches that I attributed to the lack of sleep, a rash that I blamed on a food allergy, backaches that I assumed was due to lifting weights at the gym, and forgetfulness I blamed on my unmanageable workload in my job as a CEO at a charity. All the signs that I didn't realise at the time that were leading to a devastating and life-changing outcome.

At thirty-nine, I was happily married (and gratefully I still am) and had three beautiful children, a house we had recently renovated, and I was super fit and feeling really good about myself.

I had worked my butt off literally to get myself in shape for this birthday party and standing on the steps of my house in this fitted red dress, I was feeling good. I gave an emotional speech about how blessed I was and how life had been so good to me.

I remember looking around the room and feeling content, proud and grateful of this beautiful life I had created for myself.

I had a wonderful job, great friends and an incredible family. Life was perfect.

Photos taken that night showed a happy, confident, extremely fit Linda who was embracing life and all it stood for.

I am grateful for that night of carefree indulgence and celebration, with people I loved greatly and deeply. Some of whom would soon leave me and others who would carry me through the darkest days of my life.

Less than two months after my fortieth birthday, I contracted a life-threatening illness, which meant that I was no longer able to work at my job that I loved so much.

A virus had impacted on my brain, which resulted in me being hospitalised. I was unable to work or exercise, and I was bedridden for a long period of time. For an overscheduled, highly motivated workaholic, this sudden change of lifestyle was devastating.

Not long after my illness commenced, Mum and Dad would regularly come from Wagga to Wollongong to help me in my recovery. Both Mum and Dad had recently retired after owning a pub in Hay, New South Wales, for years.

When Mum was staying with me, I noticed that she was slowing down. I would catch her having a nap during the day or taking her daily walk a bit slower. Mum was the type of person that never sat still and worked at twice the rate of everyone else, so I was pleased to see her starting to relax.

Nothing could have prepared our family for what happened next.

Dealing With Loss

Twelve months later, my beautiful Mum passed away after a very short illness. She had aggressive cancer.

My world was now in freefall, and all that I knew was rapidly spinning out of control. Having lost my job, my health and now Mum, my life had become almost unrecognisable. This was no longer the life that I had so confidently spoke about not that many months ago.

However, even with all of this, I had no idea that in just a few years my life would be completely changed again.

In 2012 my beautiful, so greatly loved daughter Molly aged thirteen was killed in an accident on our property.

My world stopped.

In an instant, not only did my life change forever but so too for her dad, devoted brother and sister, and close family and friends. The ripple of grief, shock and pain spread out to her school, her sporting groups, and the rest of the Illawarra and across Australia.

How do you keep going and living after such great loss?

How do you face each day when your world as you knew it no longer exists?

When all you want to do is give up and say I am not strong enough, I can't do this?

I need my mum, I want my daughter, and it doesn't matter how much you scream and cry, they just aren't there.

When you cry so much you vomit, and you fall to your knees with the pain and the burden of carrying your grief.

How?

Sitting With the Pain

Every person will have their own way of coping with tragedy, obstacles and loss.

For me, I just sat. I don't mean literally sitting (although there were many times I did just actually sit with a cuppa in my hand on the veranda, with my dog Sofia by my side, and just did nothing). I sat with my emotions.

With the grief, with the pain, with my sadness.

Sitting, feeling, accepting and reflecting.

Because that was an important part of my journey following the tragedy, loss and devastation.

When we get to sit with pain, we give ourselves time to try to work out how this pain, this unbearable pain, is going to find a place in your heart and in your life.

So often we are forced to run from the pain and the loss and return to our previous life too quickly. This may be due to financial pressure, family responsibilities or even a fear of having to sit and feel.

But in the sitting, I had the beginning of transformation. It was the start of laying the foundation from which my new life was to be built.

I sat for a long time, and I think you need to let yourself sit for however long it takes, at your own pace and ignore the well-meaning people that tell you to just be strong and move on. This is your journey, and you must find your way to navigate it.

I have learnt so much in the "just sitting". It gave me time to understand this new life that awaited me. My life looked different now, and although I wanted to replace the lenses that had changed how my world looked, I could not. Just like how the eyes need time to adapt when you enter a dark room, I needed time to allow my heart and soul to also adapt and accept this new view in front of me.

Sitting also allows time to understand and accept the obstacles that will lie ahead. When tragedy or loss happens, it can change you and that is something that requires time to accept.

After Molly's death, I just needed time to get to know myself and my family all over again, and in turn others had to get to know the new me. I was not the same person as before, nor could I expect to be, so time allowed me to find a way to get to know myself all over again.

Sitting also gives you time to pay respect and honour all those new emotions you are feeling – feelings that were new and foreign. This was the time I needed to integrate this catastrophic loss into my life. Some people may throw themselves into work and use this structured familiar routine as their time to process and rebuild.

Then when you are ready, you take the next step.

Just like a baby learning to walk, you may need a helping hand with your first step. You may need to be picked up and carried for a bit longer, you may only just manage to crawl.

But you are moving.

Bit by bit.

Still carrying the pain, but slowly getting used to the weight and feel of it.

Simply Showing Up

There will be times when you put up your hand up and say, "Hey, I need some help here", and tap into a network of support that is ready and waiting. Remember, we are all hardwired to support each other.

Asking for help can be difficult, so allowing people to offer support and help can be very brave yet confronting. Other times you do not even know what help you need, so that is when showing up as a friend to someone who is having challenges is one of the best gifts you can give.

I remember there were times when I didn't even know what kind of help, I needed, but I knew that my shoulders were weary from the burden of carrying my pain and the pain of others, and I needed another set of shoulders to help carry the load. Sometimes I just needed someone to sit with me, to remind me that I still had a life beyond my loss.

The power of kindness and friendships can never be underestimated.

When we see someone struggling, it is so important to reach out. So many people are facing daily obstacles, and they may just need one person to let them know that they are there to help, to walk beside them and even help carry the emotional burden. That one moment in time that person can get some relief may be the respite they need to take the next step.

Even the smallest thing can make the difference to someone. Amid the tragedy of Molly's death, I was constantly reminded of just how wonderful people can be.

I would not have made it to a life of clarity, purpose, love and joy without the unwavering support and love from family and friends.

Help can show up in so many ways. It is so hard sometimes to know what to do when someone is hurting but showing up in some way can make all the difference in that moment of time for that person.

In the early days of tragedy, a person can be incredibly vulnerable and making even the simplest decision can be difficult. Someone who can help make the decision of what meal to prepare, what needs washing or what bills need to be paid can make a huge difference.

Having Gratitude

Overcoming obstacles and transformation after great loss is not a linear pattern. It will not be a straight path from A to B.

The journey will take twists and turns, but you can do this – at your pace. And as the journey continues, you learn from each step what works for you and what doesn't. The people who start the journey with you may not be there further along, but that's alright as just like in a relay race, they pass the baton on to the next person to help accompany you.

At different steps along the way, there will be a new roadblock or a new tree blocking the path, but this time instead of feeling helpless and unsure of what to do, you know how to reroute, or just sit and wait calmly while the road ahead becomes clear again.

Each step along the way will bring more clarity, more struggles but more gratitude for a life that is still being lived. Despite the catastrophic losses I have experienced, I am still living a life of joy, hope and happiness.

Gratitude is part of my daily routine and the days when I am catapulted back into pain and loss, I use the power of gratitude even more. I am grateful for my husband, my children, my animals, my business, my friends and my latest Netflix show.

Having gratitude encourages a deep and profound appreciation of all that life offers. When I am grateful, my heart and soul are in alignment, and the world becomes a much nicer place for me. I feel an energetic change and I am more connected to my world than before. It fills my heart and my head and allows me to have respite from the pain and loss.

There has been much research into the benefits of gratitude. Gratitude can make us happier and healthier; it strengthens our emotions and makes us more optimistic and hopeful. The darker the days, the more I miss Molly, the more I seek gratitude.

Being Present

There are still many times that I choose to sit and allow the pain and all that it brings.

Being present was also another important part of how I overcome obstacles.

Being present means living in the moment. For me that meant giving myself permission to stay in the moment, allowing thoughts to come and go without letting my mind race ahead.

If I was doing something I loved, I only allowed myself to stay with that activity, engaging in conversations with every part of me, listening, watching and communicating. By living in the moment, I can achieve a place of calmness and gratitude.

By slowing down my pace of life, I now have time to notice the details I have previously missed and never had the opportunity to appreciate.

I have also learnt the importance of good old-fashioned self-care. Eating the right foods, trying to get enough sleep and being physically active can all greatly contribute to or detract from your ability to cope. These all seem so basic, but it is amazing how easy it is to lose the value of these fundamentals.

Through my attempts to harness every strategy to cope, I learnt about the power of gut health. What and how you eat can directly impact on your behaviour, mental health, immunity and energy levels.

Facing grief or overcoming loss of any kind is a monumental task and is exhausting. The number of strategies needed daily are never ending. Changing the way I ate was probably one of the easiest strategies I used, yet one that many people underestimate for its impact.

There were some immediate benefits. I started to sleep more evenly, my grief somehow softened and I had less highs and lows. When we don't get enough sleep, it impacts our immune system, our mood and our ability to handle everyday responsibilities. It can make everything seem more difficult. I now recognise the link between what I eat and drink, and how I feel and sleep.

Moving Forward

I am learning all the time about the ebbs and flows of life after loss. But I am still moving forward. Navigating obstacles, clearing paths and even creating new pathways for others to follow.

The goal posts keep moving, but in a good way. At first, I wanted to be able to set a goal of getting out of bed and getting dressed. This may seem very simple, but the reality was that it was difficult. Staying at home in bed in my PJs kept me protected from the world and reality. It easily became a safe place. Sometimes too safe, and I was reluctant to make any efforts to leave this haven.

Once I managed that, then my next goal was to try to leave the house and eventually recommence social activity. This required lots of support and reassurance from family and friends.

As I became accustomed to this life and was beginning to regain my footing, my goals would change again. My goals change as my journey continues, and they reflect the steps and the progress I have made.

Now my goal is to have my book (*Crawling Through the Darkness*) on resilience and grief published and become a motivational speaker while I continue to grow our business, Poseidon Animal Health. I would never have imagined in those early days of grief and loss that one day I would transform my love of horse and knowledge of gut health into a very successful business.

In a short time, Poseidon Equine, which is part of Poseidon Animal Health that I run with my husband, has become a leader in equine gut health, and we have just launched into the canine area. Horses and dogs played such a big part in my processing of grief. My business is my way of giving back to them.

I have now created an authentic life that allows me to do what I love. I embrace each day, and life has taught me that as clichéd as it may sound, life is short and not to be taken for granted. Every day is a gift, and everyone has a different road to walk but each step can bring wonderment and joy as well as sadness and pain.

Conclusion

One day, however far away it is, you will stop, pause, breathe and then turn to look at how far you have come and how much you have learnt about yourself on the way.

And when that day happens, you will be in awe of the brilliance, the sheer colours and magnitude of this new life and view.

And you will understand that despite all that life will throw at you, not only will you survive but you can still live a life of purpose, engagement and clarity. Frustration, pain, sadness, joy, happiness, curiosity and so on can all co-exist. They can all teach something. How can we truly appreciate joy if we haven't experienced pain or loss?

Through my journey of loss and grief, I learnt so much about myself. I experienced loss in so many ways, including my health and employment, and it was through these challenges that I learnt so much about myself and what I was and wasn't capable of.

These are insights I might never have had if my life had played out differently. I would give anything to have Molly and Mum back living alongside me, but I am forever grateful for the lessons learnt and the gift of valuing life they have given me.

I know that as time continues, there will be more obstacles, more challenges and more lessons, but equally there will be more joy, love and awe.

And that is life.

A life that I want to embrace and enjoy for all that it offers and will continue to do so.

About the Author

Linda Goldspink-Lord is a powerful presenter and an advocate for resilience and growth. Her own complex experiences in life, family and career have led her to a place of great understanding and awareness. As someone who is driven to educate others, Linda is determined to share her own life-changing experiences, as a way of empowering her audience.

From chief executive of a not-for-profit organisation at just 22, to coping with her own health crisis, traumatic family loss and intense grief, to today, as the founder of Australia's fastest-growing animal gut health company, Linda's journey has been full of highs, lows and huge opportunities for personal growth.

After collapsing with encephalitis in 2007 and struggling with major health issues, Linda was then utterly floored by the death of her mother, and then the tragic loss of her daughter Molly in an accident in 2012.

The path to recovery and acceptance has been rocky, but with support from her family, comfort from her much-loved horses and dogs, and determination to learn and grow, Linda has come out the other side, and harnessed her energy and resilience to build a life on her own terms.

Today, Linda is a passionate advocate for resilience and healing after loss and is committed to sharing her own story of overcoming major obstacles, to help other people who might be facing similar challenges.

Chapter Four
The Importance of Community and How to Find It

By Clare Doye
Direct Virtual Consulting

Seeking Connection in Rural and Regional Australia

Connection, community and belonging – it is a basic human desire that is instilled within us from our ancestors. Studies have also shown that people with strong social connections may live longer, healthier and happier lives.

We all long to have that feeling of acceptance and belonging in all areas of our lives. For some people it is a lifelong journey and for others it seems to come easily.

Positive social connectivity with people and groups releases oxytocin and serotonin, which activates the striatum area of the brain responsible for the rewards system. This in turn increases the desire for more social interaction.

There are many factors that impact how we look for this connection in our day-to-day lives including socioeconomic status, such as income, employment, education and economic wellbeing; access to suitable healthcare such as mental health services; and even your vices can play a part.

For those people who are in a less favourable socioeconomic situation, it can be much harder to find social connections that are beneficial, meaningful and helpful, and this becomes even more difficult within rural and regional communities.

This points out the disparity in opportunities within our communities, even though Australia is a resource-rich country, we need to put more time, energy and resources into creating, supporting and offering more opportunities in rural and regional areas.

When we are faced with situations in our lives that test us, such as illness, injury, grief or trauma, the importance of having a support network to rely on cannot be underestimated. Similarly, when you are going through your happiest times, having people to share your triumphs and celebrate with you can make this experience even more special.

Everyone deserves to know what it feels like to belong, to be a part of something important that you are passionate about. In a podcast, author and inspirational speaker Simon Sinek said, "Humans are social animals. We seek belonging. We feel safer in a tribe than alone. But not all tribes are healthy." So, how do we find our tribe, our special place in the community, regardless of where that community lies?

Living in the city or metropolitan areas in Australia rewards you with many options for growth and advancing your career and business. The sheer volume of the population means that generally there is always something happening that you can access including courses, workshops and opportunities for entertainment and connection with like-minded people.

Not only are there a lot more options, you can also choose based on what suits your business, lifestyle and outcomes you want to achieve.

Rural living, however, has many challenges, we face harsh climates, long distances from vital health services and a general lack of support and options for all residents. Tangentially, it can also be an absolutely beautiful place to live, raise families and grow thriving businesses, if you can get the right support. We have to create opportunities for ourselves or settle for less suitable options.

In saying this, throughout the duration of the Covid-19 outbreak, we have definitely fared better than our metropolitan and city counterparts, with less lockdowns, less outbreaks of cases and increased freedom. We watched as other areas suffered, and for the first time, our isolation was a benefit to us.

Breaking the Traditional Mould

Starting a business can be a time of great joy, excitement and motivation, but it can also be scary, leaving you feeling isolated and alone. Everyone has different needs when it comes to feeling supported, for some they might need minimal guidance and others may need more in-depth guidance, especially if they have never run a business before.

For women who are based in rural locations, it can be even more difficult, but with advances in technology, information and community are more readily accessible than before.

According to The Australian Bureau of Statistics, women now account for over a third, or 34% (668,670 women), of all business operators. This is an increase of 46% over the past twenty years. The increase in the number of men setting up their own business over the same time period was 27%.[3]

Growing up in Inverell, my mum worked since I was in late primary school, and Dad ran his own business for years (he made it look like really brutal, hard work). I would say that I never thought it was possible to start my own business until I

---

3 - https://www.thehippocket.com.au/the-number-of-female-entrepreneurs-in-australia-is-growing/#:~:text=Women%20now%20account%20for%20over,time%20was%2027%20per%20cent

was in my thirties. What would I do within the business? Do I have skills that I can offer people? Was my idea good enough?

Throughout my twenties I worked in many roles and always felt successful but never fulfilled. I had great skills, I was good with people and enjoyed working in administration roles. I rarely met women who were in high-level management positions or running their own businesses, and there are no women in my family running their own businesses.

You know what they say, you mirror what you see growing up. I worked in traditional roles, started feeling flat, changed jobs, felt invigorated for a while and then the cycle started all over again.

Something was missing but how do you know what it is?

I tried travelling, lived in all sorts of places both city and regional, went overseas and eventually returned home to my rural hometown of Inverell. I continued working and looking for the answer, luckily for me it came to me by chance – that's how it happens sometimes.

I started my virtual assistant business in 2019 alongside my traditional roles and gradually built it up to a point where I felt comfortable letting go and going full-time in my own business. I could build my business online, work the hours I wanted to, travel if I felt like it with minimal impact and earn what I wanted as well.

I also started meeting other women working in businesses and building their own empires, and I started to really feel like I was onto something. It has taken a mix of determination, confidence and trust in myself to get to this point, a man would have perhaps just done it, no problem and without question.

We have a long way to go before women have an equally fair chance at success as men do. Women account for approximately 34% of business owners in Australia, this equates to around

12% of the employed female population. Why are women not so readily willing or able to start businesses?

There are many reasons including starting and raising families, limited access to educational support and guidance, perceived gender roles or societal norms, lacking self-confidence and a perceived shortage of skills.

Also, if you are living in a community where you are not born and raised it can be difficult to make close connections and friendships as the community can be unknowingly cliquey.

Where do you turn for guidance and support?

What if you have an idea but need to know if it is a viable option?

How can you build and grow your business while maintaining those connections?

How can we actively promote and support more women to take the leap and start their own businesses for the benefit of themselves and their families, not to mention their communities?

How do women learn to lean into their power to create their own success?

How do we go about building, creating and growing our community to ensure that there is enough support in all areas?

Even starting the conversation is a huge step in finding the answers we need to succeed.

Finding Your *Why*

Initially, it is beneficial to do some introspection on who you are, social connections work best when you show up as your authentic self. It is important to foster a loving relationship with yourself, this can take time as there is often some past conditioning that we have to work through to reach this point.

You must also be clear on what your goals are (both personal and business), your business style, your audience and what sort of needs you feel are not being met. Find your *why*. It might be helpful to create a purpose statement that describes why you do the work that you do, why you live the lifestyle you do and what is your mission, your goals and your vision.

Women often find the meaning behind their business has quite an emotive story or at least this makes up a large portion of the business, the passion behind their business story drives them and encourages them to thrive and grow. Finding the answers to these questions allow you to seek connections and groups that are relevant to you and your values.

Jim Rohn, who is a self-made millionaire and motivational speaker, famously said, "You are the average of five people you spend the most time with." While this quote is not entirely true, those around you can have a significant impact on your life.

You're not looking for people who fill the gaps within yourself, you're looking for complementary personalities who challenge you in a positive way to expand yourself and broaden your mind.

You also have to release the judgement of yourself and others, it can be quite hard to achieve, imposter syndrome has a way of raising its ugly head repeatedly. You want to be open to meeting new people and accepting advice and creative criticism where required, these things are difficult to do if you are stuck in a bad mindset.

I find that a mindful approach helps to overcome imposter syndrome. You should reflect on the rationale behind your feelings. Generally, we are comparing ourselves with others who are doing similar things to us but often we are comparing ourselves with people who are doing completely different things.

You cannot compare your journey with that of another person, you don't know how far they have come, the reality they are living in or the struggles they are facing. Focus on you, stay in your own lane, make your goals and achieve them – it is the only way to keep imposter syndrome at bay and ultimately beat it at its own game.

As the queen of personal development Brené Brown said in her podcast, "True belonging only happens when we present our authentic, imperfect selves to the world. Our sense of belonging can never be greater than our sense of self-acceptance."

Making the Connection

One of the main issues facing women in business, especially those in rural and regional areas, is the seeming lack of like-minded community connections that are easily accessible.

While we are often living hours from the nearest city, the internet is now so advanced that we barely notice a lag in our ability to connect with people all over the world – we are able to gain the connection we felt was lacking. We are not so cut off from the rest of the country and the world anymore.

We can have face-to-face meetings with people, make new business connections, interview for roles we might never have had access to. However, it sometimes leaves us with a connection void in another area. If you're running a business, it is often with fellow business owners, especially women.

The easiest way to make connections within your community is to network – yet you might find that there is a lack of networking groups in your area. These groups create a sense of community, purpose and structure that is so often missing in rural and regional areas and can create lifelong friendships.

I did some market research within my business community and the number one issue facing women is the inability to fit networking into their week, alongside raising children, working on/in their businesses and maintaining relationships with their significant others and families, leaving them feeling pulled in too many directions.

There is also difficulty finding niche networking opportunities when their business is unique or slightly different, many women find themselves seeking connections beyond their own community, using online options.

Those surveyed also stated that networking is one of the main areas they felt they needed ongoing support for within their business, followed by mindset and ongoing learning and training opportunities.

What do you do if there is no suitable networking group within your local community?

Why not take the leap and start your own – you don't have to limit it to just women in business, even women who work within the community or women who might like to run a business in the future.

Things to consider when starting your own group could be:

- Define the purpose of the group
- Decide the format you would like the group to follow. Will it be a formal or informal event?
- Will it be a free or paid group?
- Create a Facebook page and promote it in areas that are relevant to your purpose

Networking, both formal and casual, allows women to talk about all facets of their lives, to take up space where they feel safe among peers who truly understand them and their unique struggles. This is when women truly shine and the support and understanding that comes from these meetings cannot be underestimated.

Don't be afraid to create the space you need to flourish, call out to your local community, throw caution to the wind and value yourself and your ideas enough to take up space.

Two women together, sharing information, skills, knowledge and offering each other support and encouragement is always better than doing it alone. You will feel more powerful and capable if you have the support behind you to push you to the next level.

If you are not quite ready yet to do in-person networking you could try online networking groups, these often give you the kick-off you need and can be great because you're a little bit anonymous within these groups. It often happens that you will be the only person in your area within the group, so you may feel more comfortable sharing some ideas or getting feedback.

These groups are often more heavily niched. If you're looking for a networking group that is very specific, you're sure to find something. Where online networking doesn't always create the connections you need or foster the understanding of your unique situation, often a mix of in-person and online events can strike a really nice balance.

Social media has opened up a whole new world in terms of connections, both business and personal. Some people are finding themselves simultaneously more connected and isolated and, at the same time, we have almost unfettered access to each other. We can now be connected virtually to close friends, family, acquaintances, business connections and even strangers.

Sometimes we feel so connected that we forget about actively connecting to those we love, we know all the details of their lives because it is all laid out for us to read every day. It is so important that we use technology as a tool and not to replace meaningful connections.

Making Mindful Connections

Have you often found yourself mindlessly scrolling through social media, speed reading what everyone else is up to, seeing the mostly "perfect" lives they present to the rest of the world?

There is a serious shortage of real conversation in many people's lives, they keep up to date with people by reading their status updates and looking at their pictures, instead of having meaningful conversations.

I believe that we need to take a mindful approach to our social media use, actively engaging with those we cannot easily see in-person and not following anyone and everyone.

How do we use social media mindfully?

- Consider your objectives before you open the app. Why are you opening the app, do you have an intention you would like to achieve?

- Present yourself authentically in your own posts. We don't enjoy other people falsely representing themselves on social media, so let's set a standard for what we prefer and expect.

- Don't just mindlessly scroll, interact and connect with others! Get online and direct message or call those you consider most important to you. Create a space for meaningful conversations with each other in a genuine way.

- Avoid following people or companies who bring negative vibes to your feed, this goes without explanation, really. Those negative feelings can follow you throughout your day and ruin moments that would have otherwise been wonderful.

- Allow yourself to be bored sometimes, bored is healthy and good for you as it provides an opportunity for introspection and reflection. It can also encourage the mind to be more creative and to daydream, which is a really lovely way for your mind to have a break and refresh.

- Turn off your notifications (I found this immediately took away a lot of my anxiety), without the constant noise of notifications coming through, you will start to look less at your device and be able to focus more on important things (like daydreaming). Always remember, if it was something important, they would call you!

Use these tips to start new habits for yourself and those around you, especially kids. Social media has seen a marked increase in depression and suicide rates among a very vulnerable section of our population – teenagers.

Loneliness stems from the feeling that you are lacking in quality relationships in your life – anyone can feel this way. We need more meaningful connections in our lives and less shallow ones, and we must be patient and consistent in our pursuit of these connections.

As Brené Brown said, "I define connection as the energy that exists between people when they feel seen, heard and valued; when they can give and receive without judgment; and when they derive sustenance and strength from the relationship."

Conclusion

It is wonderful to have the option of in-person and virtual connection, the key is to actively seek it and engage with others to grow that connection with others that can help to support us in our journey.

How will you be changing the way you do things in your own life to create these meaningful connections?

Do you have a community that fulfills your needs when it comes to your business?

There is no right or wrong way to create the community you need to help you succeed in business, we are all doing the best we can, looking for tools we can use to take us further and give us the balance we crave.

About the Author

Clare Doye grew up in Inverell NSW and moved away at about 20 to explore the country, even working in Canada for a short stint, before returning to Inverell in 2015 to be closer to family.

Inverell truly is a beautiful place to live and ironically, Clare ended up meeting her partner there. They grew up in similar circles and still did not meet until she returned. Clare lives with her partner, dog and cat and an enormous number of indoor plants.

Running a business is a relatively new concept for Clare since starting Direct Virtual Consulting in 2019 (after 16 years in administration roles). She wanted to work with established business owners who know they need support and were excited to grow their business.

Clare's passion for helping others is evident when she finds like-minded people.

In her spare time Clare runs an art business called Colourbliss Studio where she uses resin and alcohol inks to create artworks. She loves having the ability to channel her energy into creating beauty in the world.

Clare also loves listening to true crime podcasts and watching crime dramas.

Chapter Five
Building Psychological Flexibility to Build Your Business and Thrive in Adversity

By Stephanie Schmidt
ACT for Ag

Have you ever experienced discomfort, anxiety, frustration, worry, uncertainty or anger? Have you ever had a voice in your mind say, "I'm not good enough. I can't do this. Everyone is better at this than me. No one wants to hear what I have to say"?

I have. Even just as I sit down to write down this chapter, I have experienced all the above.

Why does that happen, when writing this chapter is something that is important to me, something that I value? Why is it that my mind makes it so hard to write? We can start with a bit of an understanding of why our mind does what it does.

Psychologists and social scientists suggest that our human mind has evolved with two main priorities. First is to keep us safe and alive. Second is to make sure we fit in with our social group. Keeping ourselves connected to our social group is deeply linked to keep us alive – without social connections, we die. So, as human beings we are completely driven to connect to our social group.

As a result, our cavewoman brains became experts at looking out for things that may be dangerous or may threaten our connection to our group. Our minds became experts at predicting danger, thinking about things that may be dangerous, replaying dangerous situations and avoiding dangers.

The better your ancestors were at looking out for danger, the more likely they were to survive and produce offspring, and the more likely you are to be standing here, reading this right now.

We have inherited this problem-solving, comparing, predicting and avoiding mindset from our ancestors. We have these minds that are primed for worrying, replaying difficult or stressful things that have happened, predicting the worst and comparing ourselves to others to make sure we "fit in" to the group.

As I sit down to write this chapter, my mind foresees all sorts of potential dangers, especially when it comes to fitting in with my social group. My mind starts telling me all kinds of stories, "Don't do it, they'll find out you're a fraud. You're an imposter, everyone else is so much smarter than you. You don't have the time, and if you are going to do it, you better make it perfect."

To get away from those uncomfortable thoughts and feelings that come along for the ride, such as anxiety, worry, frustration and shame, I avoid.

I avoid taking the small steps towards writing this chapter because that keeps me safe. The act of avoiding keeps me in the comfort zone and away from danger.

But, at the same time, it keeps me away from doing some of what I value most – showing up, sharing knowledge to help others manage challenging situations, and taking on new challenges for myself.

How do you move towards what matters most to you – even with all the challenging stuff your mind throws at you along the way?

Keep in mind that as you work through this chapter, change happens in the practice, not just knowledge of these skills and ideas. Try out the exercises or pick one exercise to try on for size. Focus on it for a day or week and see what happens.

This is not just a chapter to read, but to **do** as well. Work through it in a way that fits you, either bit by bit, go through each exercise one by one, or read through the entire chapter and then work through the exercises. There is no right or wrong way, but importantly, just **do** something, don't just read about it.

Our Cavewoman Brain – Why We Do What We Do and Get Stuck Where We Get Stuck

We are lucky to inherit our cavewoman brains from our ancestors – brains that are wired to keep us safe, look out for danger and make sure we don't do anything that may damage our safety within our social group. We are also wired to connect with others and seek safety through that connection.

Like all animals, we have survived by moving away from things that may be dangerous and moving towards safety and things that are important to us (shelter, food and social connection).

One key difference between humans and animals is our capacity for language. With language, we can create a rich inner world and give names and labels to our outside experiences. Language gives us the ability to solve problems, plan, create and use mental time travel to move between the past, present and future.

This is an incredibly helpful skill and strength. However, if left unchecked we often tend to get stuck in our minds – hooked by our thoughts and removed from what is actually happening in the present moment.

Psychological flexibility is being able to be present in this moment right now, to hold lightly to the difficult thoughts and feelings that show up, and adapt our actions and choices based on what is most important to us, choosing to take actions that move us towards our values.

The Noticing Map – A Map to Build Flexibility

There are a lot of tools, strategies and exercises that can help us build psychological flexibility – many of them founded in acceptance and commitment therapy (ACT), as well as other evidence-based approaches such as compassion-focused therapy and mindfulness training.

One tool, which can be used as a foundation for building your flexibility every day, is the noticing map, which is adapted from the ACT matrix, originally developed by psychologists Kevin Polk, Benjamin Schoendorff and colleagues, and adapted by Paul Atkins and colleagues at Prosocial World.

In the following pages, you will find a blank template and a completed example of the noticing map (adapted from the Prosocial noticing map).

The noticing map provides us with a different lens or point of view to look at our experiences. Overall, the noticing map provides us with a simple yet very effective way to look at:

- Who and what matters most to us (even during times of stress and adversity).
- How we would like to show up in the world as a human being, and what actions we can take to move towards that.

- Some of the uncomfortable and challenging stuff that can hook us and get in the way of how we would like to be, and some of the things that we tend to do when we become hooked.

Like any map, it can help you during tough times to find the next direction and the next best step to take. It is a tool that can be used to review previous events and see what you might do differently next time, to plan future events, or with practice to be able to work through the questions in your mind in present moment difficult situations.

It is a tool for developing psychological flexibility, which in a nutshell, is a set of skills that help us move towards what matters most to us – even when the tough stuff shows up.

Humans, like all animals, are driven to move towards what's important to them and move away from things that may be painful, dangerous or unpleasant. We move towards food, safety and connection with other people, and away from things that may cause us harm (snakes, hot stoves and lions).

Humans also have an additional capacity of language – the capacity to create words and meaning, which allows us to create images and ideas of the past and future. This means that we can create two worlds. First is the world of our inner experiences (our thoughts, feelings, memories, sensations and stories) and second is the outside world, what we can sense with our five senses.

You can use the noticing map to work through any situation by asking yourself:

1. Who and what matters most to me in this situation?
    a. What really matters to me about how I respond to this?
    b. How do I want to be as a person?

3. In an ideal world, if I was really living in line with what matters in [1], what would I be doing (what would a fly on the wall see me doing)?

4. What inner stuff, thoughts and feelings might show up to get in the way of me moving towards who and what really matters to me?

5. When I get hooked on the tricky stuff in my mind, what might people see me doing?
    a. How well do these strategies work (how workable are they) in the short and long term?

In the centre of this map, we have ourselves, noticing and observing – we can practice this skill in noticing and observing our own experiences and the actions of others in a kind and curious manner.

Finally, since it is inevitable that difficult thoughts and feelings will show up, what simple steps can I put in place so I can move towards what matters, even when the tough stuff shows up?

You can look through my example of the noticing map that I completed for the situation of writing this chapter. As I was able to step back, notice and identify who and what matters most to me (helping other rural women), as well as all the tricky stuff that shows up and hooks me away from taking action, I could then identify the small steps I could take to get this chapter written and sent off!

Importantly, zooming out and treating myself with kindness as I work through the template helps me take action without getting stuck in judgement towards myself.

Try it for yourself – find the blank template at the end of this chapter (a free printout is also available on www.actforag.com.au).

Think of a situation in your life right now that is mildly challenging – it doesn't need to be the most challenging thing you are facing right now as you start to learn this new skill. Work through the template by asking yourself the questions above.

As you do this, notice what you experience and observe the sensations and feelings in your body. As you note down what actions you can take to move towards what really matters to you, start straight away by taking action on one of those things, today, right now. Yes – put the book down and take action!

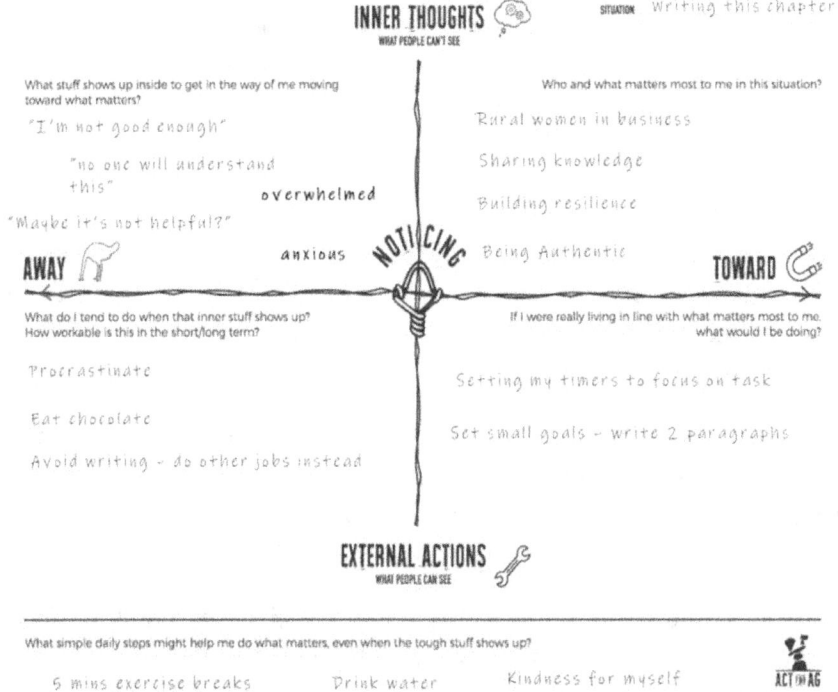

Shared Purpose Map

The beauty of the noticing map is that we can easily adapt it to look at how to move towards what matters most for a group – this may be a couple, a family, a business or a community group. Find a template and example of the shared purpose map at www.actforag.com.au. – the key change is to notice *what matters most to **us** in this situation? What is **our** shared purpose?*

Strengthening Your Skills in Psychological Flexibility

As well as using the noticing and shared purpose maps to work through and build your psychological flexibility, we can also strengthen three core psychological flexibility skills: noticing skills, openness skills and action skills.

As described, psychological flexibility is about noticing and being aware of our present experience; be open to difficult thoughts and feelings and hold them lightly; and to take action towards our values.

Noticing Skills

Noticing skills are about strengthening your awareness of yourself and others. They also involve techniques to be able to practice being in and experience the present moment, non-judgementally.

Our mind is a fantastic time traveller – it can replay difficulties from the past, or predict potential challenges or dangers in the future. However, we can start by being present and checking in to ask ourselves, "Where is my mind right now?"

While noticing and awareness sounds simple, we live in a world where we are constantly faced with distraction and interruption. Our mind attempts to multitask and think about a lot of things at once. When our mind is scattered, it becomes ineffective.

Building noticing skills is essentially a form of mental training. Increasing your ability to be present and aware of what's happening in the present moment, while also remaining non-judgemental, can help you to switch off your autopilot and build your ability to strengthen your scattered mind.

Noticing skills can be developed in three key ways:

- Becoming more aware during your daily routine activities
- Having regular noticing "check-ins" throughout the day
- Doing regular guided practices

Noticing Skills in Our Daily Activities

You can start to build your noticing and awareness muscle by practicing switching off autopilot while you go about your daily activities. You may choose to practice building your noticing skills while you take an action that is important to you, for example while you play with your kids.

You can also practice your noticing skills during those daily routines that we tend to do on autopilot, such as having a cup of coffee, cleaning your teeth, having a shower and driving.

See if you can bring mindful attention to these daily activities and notice what you experience. Think about one or two of the things you regularly do on autopilot and practice engaging your noticing skills during this activity over the next week.

You may find it helpful to have a sticky note with the words "Notice" or "Switch Off Autopilot" or something that fits for you as a reminder!

Noticing "Check-Ins"

Throughout the day practice briefly checking in with yourself. This can simply be done by pausing for a moment and asking, "Where is my mind right now?" Is it here in the present moment, or is it time travelling to the past or future?

You can also practice switching off autopilot and engaging with your immediate environment by practicing the five senses exercise:

5-4-3-2-1 Practice Noticing:

- 5 things you can see
- 4 things you can feel/touch
- 3 things you can hear
- 2 things you can smell
- 1 thing you can taste

This can also be a useful exercise to practice when you need to unhook from tricky or uncomfortable thoughts and feelings in your mind.

Again, it can be difficult to create new habits. So, try popping sticky note reminders around the house with "Where is my mind right now?", "Get present", or "Be here now". Even pop a reminder in your phone to *ding* and remind you a couple of times each day.

Regular Guided Practices

In the same way that you wouldn't turn up to play a game of footy without going to practice or run a marathon without training first, regular noticing practice helps us strengthen our "attention" and noticing muscles.

There are a wide range of tools available to do this, for example apps such as Smiling Mind, Headspace and Calm. Below is a script for a simple, mindful breathing exercise, you can read through the script and then practice yourself.

You will also find a recording of the exercise in the resources at *www.actforag.com.au*. Like anything, when you are learning a new skill, it's helpful to have some guidance along the way.

***

Mindful Breathing

Our breath is something we have with us all the time. We can use it simply and easily to practice building our noticing and awareness muscles.

This can be done in any situation, you might practice taking three to five mindful breaths, or if you find it beneficial, you can pop on a timer and practice mindful breathing for five minutes, or link in and use one of the audio exercises online to help you practice.

Close your eyes if you are comfortable.

Bring your attention to your breathing. Just notice and observe the sensation of your breath flowing in and out of your body. Notice the gentle rise and fall of your shoulders, the gentle rise and fall of your chest and stomach.

Notice the breath flowing in and out of your nostrils, how your breath is slightly warmer as it flows in and slightly cooler as it flows out.

Don't try and change your breathing in anyway but just observe and notice it. Choose one of the sensations of breath in your body and focus your attention there. You may also say to yourself, "I notice I'm breathing in, I notice I'm breathing out". Or count each breath as you breathe in and out.

As you do this notice if your mind interrupts you, or if you get hooked by different thoughts and feelings – and then gently bring your awareness back to the breath.

Time and time again your mind will distract you, this is perfectly normal and natural. Just acknowledge what distracted you, thank your mind, and gently guide your attention back to your breathing.

***

Openness Skills – Strategies to Practice When the Uncomfortable Stuff Shows Up

Difficult and painful thoughts, feelings, memories and sensations are inevitable. In fact, they are human nature and vital to our experience.

Can you image what might happen if we didn't have a mind that told us about potential dangers or what might go wrong? What might happen if we had a mind that didn't replay difficulties or struggles from the past, to solve problems, how we might deal with them in the future?

What might happen if we had a mind that didn't care what other people think? A mind that didn't care whether we fitted in with our social group, our peers or our families?

Our mind has evolved to keep us safe, to keep us alive and to keep us socially connected. All these things are vital, so it makes sense that we have a mind that solves problems and compares, judges, criticises, worries and predicts the future.

Our body also gives us data on the world around us through our emotions and feelings. Anger tells us that something is wrong, fear and anxiety tells us something might be dangerous, sadness might tell us that we have lost something that matters – all our feelings are like signposts, giving us data and information about our external world.

However, when we get rigidly stuck on these thoughts and feelings, or get stuck trying to avoid these thoughts or painful feelings, we can end up being hijacked and moving away from what truly matters to us.

Openness – Holding it lightly is about learning to skilfully relate to our inner world. Instead of getting caught up and hooked by our difficult thoughts and feelings, or putting all our energy into trying to get rid of the uncomfortable stuff, we can learn to open up and hold this stuff lightly, so that our hands are free to do what really matters to us.

For the rural women who are on farms or grew up on farm, have you ever skirted sheep's wool? When we skirt the wool, we can't stop the prickles, dags and other bits from being there, but it's much more pleasant to do it with a light touch, rather than grabbing hold of prickly wool with both hands.

Holding it lightly recognises that the tough stuff is going to show up in life whether we like it or not, but with a light touch, you can sort through thoughts, feelings and sensations that come up under your skin, and choose to hold on to those that help and let go of those that don't.

Building Skills to Hold It Lightly With Openness

These skills are techniques that help us to better relate to our thoughts, feelings, urges and moods – all the stuff that as humans, we have going on inside of us most of the time.

Our mind can be like a never-ending live commentary of everything that is happening in our lives – a livestream of judgements, observations, criticisms, worry, predictions and replays.

Instead of putting your energy into trying to stop or change those thoughts, which at times can be like engaging in an unwinnable battle, we can learn to change our relationship with the stuff that shows up in our minds.

Creating Space Between Our Thoughts and Ourselves

At times our thoughts can hook us in, we get trapped into believing that our thoughts are true or real. They can hijack us and take us away from what's important to us. We don't need to get into an argument with our thoughts to try to prove them wrong or even buy into them completely.

Alternatively, we try to put our energy into stopping thoughts we don't want to have. Unfortunately, purely because of the way our mind works, this can backfire. To try this out, I want you to make sure that for the next 30 seconds, you *do not think* about chocolate cake. You can think of anything at all, but whatever you do, *do not think* about chocolate cake …

How did you go? Chances are, the thought or image of a chocolate cake popped into your mind, even if only for a moment. Psychologists and researchers have found that because our mind works by creating relationships and associations, the more we try not to think about something, we prime our mind to think about it.

What we can do instead is practise making space between our thoughts and ourselves. Recognising our thoughts for exactly what they are – just thoughts/images/stories/memories that pop up in our mind – and then we can choose whether or not we engage with them.

For example, when I'm tired, frustrated or sick of my kids yelling and bickering with each other, I might eventually snap and yell at them to just be quiet. After this, my mind goes wild telling me all the ways that I'm not a good enough parent or that I'm a bad mum.

Sometimes I try to argue with my mind, convince myself of all the ways I am good enough, how much my kids push my buttons and that it's not my fault. But my mind usually wins, and in the time that I get caught up in that argument in my mind, I've wound myself up tighter and tighter, and my fuse with my kids gets shorter and shorter.

Alternatively, I get completely caught up in the thoughts, and my mind gives me all the evidence from history of all the ways that I really am a bad mum. Again, my mood plummets, my fuse gets shorter, and inevitably I end up yelling at my kids.

I can practice changing my relationship with my thoughts. Instead of trying to change, fix or buy into the negative thought, I just recognise my thoughts for what they are, "I'm having the thought that I'm not a good enough parent." I notice it, acknowledge it, then move on with what I'm doing.

I then have space to sit and play with my kids or ask them with kindness to go outside. I have the space to act in line with the person I want to be, even when difficult feelings show up.

It sounds simple but practicing *naming* our thoughts and feelings can start to change our relationship with them. Simply start to notice and recognise our thoughts and feelings just as they are – thoughts and feelings that come up in our mind – can start to give us that space to choose our actions.

This might look like saying to yourself, "I'm feeling anxious. Here is anger. I'm having the thought that this isn't fair."

Notice what difficult thoughts or feelings are coming up, then practice labelling them:

- "I'm having the thought that …"
- "My mind is telling me …"
- "The story my mind is telling me is …"
- "I'm feeling …"
- "Here is …"

As a small experiment, try it out for yourself. Think of one of the tricky or difficult thoughts that comes up for you at times, for example, I can't do this or I'm not good enough.

Notice what happens in your body as you think that thought over and over for thirty seconds or so. Then, add one of the naming tools above, for example, "I'm having the thought that I'm not good enough." Notice what happens when you think that over in your mind.

Putting It to Action – Identify What Matters Most to You

Becoming present, noticing and being open to our experiences all serve to help us be more flexible in the choices and decisions we make every day. But how do we decide what we truly want to do?

Our values act as a compass to guide our daily behaviours. Values are not about what you want to get or achieve; they are about how you want to behave or act on an ongoing basis, and how you want to treat yourself and others in the world around you. Our values are the personal qualities that we truly wish to express in our daily behaviours.

There are no "right" or "wrong" values, our values are unique to us, and our values may also flow and change, and be different in different situations.

We don't often pause and take note of what our values are, so one of the most important first steps in become active and moving towards what's most important to us is actually taking the time to explore and examine what's most important to us, and what our "why" is.

Try the following exercise to start to explore what your values may be:

Ten Years From Now

Read through and then practice the exercise for yourself

Let your eyes close gently or focus on a spot on the floor in front of you. Take a few moments to sit with the experience of your body in this room right now. Sit up straight in your chair and notice the feeling of your feet centred and grounded on the ground. Allow your face to relax into a gentle smile.

Spend a few moments noticing your breathing – notice the gentle movement of your breath flowing in and out of your body. If you find yourself distracted by your thoughts, just let go of the thoughts and bring your attention back to the breath.

Imagine yourself in ten years' time. Imagine that over the next ten years you have lived a life that is bold, you have made choices guided by what really matters to you, you have shown up and done what matters most to you – even during tough times.

Imagine where you will be, what your life will look like, what your business will look like. Imagine your ideal life and world – who would be in it, what would you be doing day to day.

Take a few moments to really picture this scene – connect with the person that is you in ten years. Notice as you do this what comes up in your body right now.

As you picture yourself in ten years' time, ask yourself, what choices have you made along the way? Who and what is most important to you? What values have you used to guide your choices and decisions?

What tricky stuff (difficult thoughts, feelings and emotions) do you need to make space for along the way, to be able to make these decisions and choices. Ultimately, what might be the same in your life, what might be different?

Take a few moments now to write down your key reflections from this exercise. What values stand out most to you? What tricky stuff might show up under your skin that you might need to make space for, or be willing to have, as you move towards your values?

There are also a number of online tools such as values lists and values sorting apps that can also help you to clarify your values.

Moving From Plans to Action

You've started to notice and identify what's most important to you, you've started to notice some of the tricky stories and feelings that come up and hook you at times – what's next?

Use SMART goals to crystalise the next step to take. Think over the exercises and work you have done from this chapter. Identify one thing you can do today and one thing you can do this week that moves you towards what really matters most to you in your business (or any life area, for example, family, health and relationships).

SMART goals can help us stay on track and take action:

Specific – Well-defined, clear and understandable

Measurable – Have specific criteria that help measure your progress towards your goal

Achievable – Not impossible but enough of a challenge to get you motivated

Realistic – Relevant to you, doable and realistic

Timely – Include a clearly defined start date and target date. This helps you stay on track and create a sense of urgency.

Instead of saying, "I'm going to get my book chapter written", you might set yourself a goal of spending two hours working on your book chapter on Wednesday or say that you will send a draft to the editors by Friday.

As you set your goal, take note on what might be some of the uncomfortable stuff that will show up inside you as you move towards that goal. Write it down and notice it. Then decide, are you willing to make space for that discomfort as you move towards what's most important to you?

Summary

Running a business is hard. Growing a business baby, building a life based on what matters most to you, finding the balance between all your needs, obligations and commitments, these are all hard.

As a rural woman, with a passion for either growing your own business or building your existing business, no doubt you have already faced many challenges along the way.

You have adapted and used flexibility, whether they have been minor, everyday challenges such as having kids home sick from school, a day when the internet goes down, or the major, big "C" challenges, like a global pandemic wiping out your income stream, a natural disaster like flood or bushfire, or the ongoing stress of drought.

Take a few moments to reflect on the skills and strengths that helped you show up with flexibility in each of those situations.

Reflect and consider whether building your psychological flexibility might help you be even more adaptable, more flexible or more effective. And ultimately, be able to adapt to the challenges that life throws at you while still holding true to what's most important to you.

The tools and skills of psychological flexibility mean that you can begin to practice showing up and doing what matters most, even when it gets tricky or tough. Your flexibility is like a muscle, you can build it and strengthen it with small steps every day.

Find one way to practice building your noticing skills in your everyday life. Find one way to practice holding on to your thoughts a little more lightly every day and find one way or one step that you can take each day to move you towards what really matters most to you.

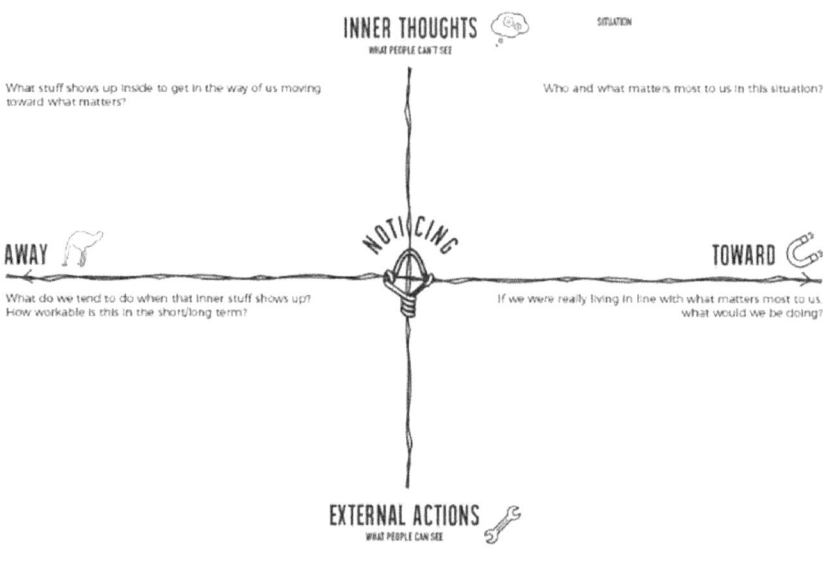

About the Author

Stephanie Schmidt: Clinical Psychologist, 2020 SA AgriFutures Rural Women's Award Winner

Growing up in suburban Adelaide, farming life was not on Steph Schmid's radar. However, when she was 19, she met her farmer, now husband, while working at The Woolshed (the country pub in the city) and life took a new direction. Steph now lives at Worlds End, South Australia with her husband and three gorgeous boys on their mixed enterprise farm (cropping and sheep). Steph is a Clinical Psychologist and was awarded the 2020 SA Agrifutures Rural Women's Award for her project – ACT for Ag.

Steph and her husband extended their farm, purchasing two properties at the start of 2018 and then were hit with the severest drought on record. This gave Steph a first-hand experience of the stress and pressure of drought. Within the farm business, Steph is responsible for managing the finances as well as assisting with extra farm jobs whenever she is able, especially at shearing, seeding, and harvest time. Steph loves spending time on the farm with her husband and sons and enjoys the privilege of being able to work together as a family. Lived experience of the challenges of farming life, managing a relationship, and raising a family, together with her psychological knowledge gives Steph unique insight. Steph is passionate about sharing her learnings and knowledge and has a vision to see a resilient rural Australia which can face the inevitable challenges and thrive in adversity.

ACT for Ag is all about building the capacity and resilience of farmers, farming families and rural communities – equipping them with easy-to-apply tools to navigate the rock and the hard place. Find out more about the work of ACT for Ag and how it may benefit you, your business or your community via the website www.actforag.com.au.

In farming and family life, Steph has learnt first-hand just how important it is to be flexible and adaptive to challenging situations. Steph developed Postnatal Depression after the birth of both her first and third sons, and through this, continues to learn the importance of looking after herself to be able to look after those around her, and to be able to live and enjoy her amazing life. Steph is passionate about sharing knowledge through story and shares her personal experiences plus reminders and strategies to stay on track via social media, check out @actforag on Instagram, Facebook and Twitter.

References – Additional Reading

Atkins, P. W.B., Wilson, D. S., and Hayes, S.C. (2019). Prosocial: Using Evolutionary Science to Build Productive, Equitable, and Collaborative Groups. Oakland, CA: Context Press.

Flaxman, P. E., Bond, F. W., & Livheim, F. (2013). The mindful and effective employee: An acceptance and commitment therapy training manual for improving well-being and performance. New Harbinger Publications.

Hayes, S. C. (2019). A liberated mind: The essential guide to ACT. London, Vermilon.

Harris, R. (2008). The Happiness Trap: How to stop struggling and start living. Boston, MA: Trumpeter.

Polk, K. L., Schoendorff, B., Webster, M., & Olaz, F. O. (2016). The essential guide to the ACT matrix: A step-by-step approach to Using the ACT matrix model in clinical practice. Oakland, CA: New Harbinger Publications.

Polk, K. L., & Schoendorff, B. (Eds.). (2014). The ACT Matrix: A New Approach to Building Psychological Flexibility Across Settings and Populations. Oakland, CA: New Harbinger Publications.

Williams, M., & Penman, D. (2011). Mindfulness: An eight-week plan for finding peace in a frantic world. Emmaus, Pa: Rodale Books.

Part 2

Getting Started

Chapter Six
How to Start an Online Business

By Sarah Britz
www.sarahbritz.com.au

Introduction

Starting a business in rural or regional Australia brings various challenges that city dwellers don't have. For those of us who live in the country, many business disadvantages can come with this lifestyle in terms of technology, logistics, potential customers and marketing.

While operating an online business has historically been much easier in a city, advances in technology have helped remove the barriers so that anyone can start and scale an online business, regardless of their location, professional background or past entrepreneurial experience.

You can now create an e-commerce store that can be accessed by potential customers anywhere and anytime with an internet connection. All you need to get started is a viable idea, an internet connection and some time to spare.

Running an online business does not have to be expensive either. There are tools and platforms out there that will allow you to set up your online business for free or at a low cost. The key is to plan and use the right tools from the beginning so that you can focus on growing your business instead of managing it.

This chapter will explain the advantages of operating an online business. It will provide an easy-to-follow overview of steps and recommendations you can take to create an easy to maintain online business that will offer you the opportunity to develop the idea to sell your products or services to customers across Australia and globally.

Why Start an Online Business?

The shift to buying products online is more apparent than ever. Australian e-commerce reached an all-time high in 2020, as the pandemic changed consumer behaviour and drove incredible growth in online shopping.

Australia Post's report, Inside Australian Online Shopping 2021, identified that 82% of Australian households are now shopping online.[4] There has never been an easier or better time to start your own business than today.

The past couple of years have shown us all that we can't take anything for granted, and things can change at the drop of a hat.

Having an online business will provide you with an income that can be sustainable through any significant disruptive event, be it bushfires, floods, pandemics, etc.

For example, before the 2019-20 bushfires, Covid-19 pandemic and lockdowns that ensued, many rural and regional small businesses were run solely as bricks-and-mortar stores. However, it took a pandemic for many of these to decide to take their operations digital and enjoy the benefits of going online.

As a result, the natural response for small businesses has been a pivot to e-commerce and a greater focus on establishing an

---

4 - https://auspost.com.au/business/marketing-and-communications/access-data-and-insights/ecommerce-trends

online presence. In addition, many small businesses have needed to move online to reach existing customers and find new customers.

These businesses previously would have had customers discover and purchase their products via foot traffic and tourism, which has been almost non-existent for many rural and regional communities in the past two years due to the impact of bushfires and lockdowns.

Therefore, the importance of creating a business that is sustainable and resilient in difficult times is more necessary now than ever.

For rural and regional small business owners, having an online business will give them the option to continue trading during difficult times. In addition, it will allow them to access and reach customers to purchase their products and services from across Australia and around the world.

Not only does having an online business allow you to target and reach a wider customer audience than a traditional business, but many traditional businesses are restricted by location and time. They can only operate out of certain geolocations and during specific hours.

On the other hand, online businesses are open 24 hours a day, 365 days a year. Therefore, a successful e-commerce store constantly attracts potential customers interested in their product from across the globe every hour of the day.

If you live in rural or regional Australia, I believe that there are many strong reasons why starting an online business is an excellent idea, these include:

- It's affordable and low cost to get started. You can now create a website inexpensively or for free. Maintenance costs of an online business are relatively low compared with the start-up and running costs of a traditional bricks-and-mortar business.

- It's flexible! You can work from anywhere and at a schedule of your choice. An online business provides the luxury of creating a work schedule that works for you.
- You can get started quickly and easily! There are many tools and resources available to get your business online and selling super fast!
- You can grow your business efficiently.
- If you have an existing business, taking your business online provides you with the most economical and efficient way to expose your business to a new and varied audience of customers and opportunities, in turn increasing your sales.

Starting an online business has many benefits, but at the same time, there are some disadvantages also to consider.

The online marketplace is competitive. While taking a business online expands your potential customer base, moving up the rankings in search engines isn't easy, especially for a new domain. Moreover, increasing your website's domain authority isn't done overnight; it takes time and effort to build credibility with Google's web crawlers.

Working from home is a dream come true for most people but not having the nine-to-five structure means working more hours. Weekends and holidays can lose meaning when working for yourself, especially if your online store is always open.

An online business will allow you to work from wherever you have internet, but many people find out quickly that doesn't translate into fewer hours. Starting a business from the ground up takes dedication that many people are not prepared for. Be sure you are ready for sleepless nights and long work weeks.

Business Requirements in Australia

Before you start or move your business online, it's essential to consider the following:

- Research online competitors to find out what works and what you could do to make your business stand out from the rest
- Find out what laws or regulations may apply to you, such as those on privacy, copyright and spam

Starting an online business in Australia is similar to a traditional company. You will need to apply for an Australian Business Number (ABN), the cost is $463 to register at the time of writing (for the latest costs, check the Australian Securities & Investments Commission [ASIC] website.) Registering the business name through ASIC will cost $37 a year or $87 every three years at the time of writing.

You will also need a domain name, which is a URL or address used online. Your domain name is a significant decision, be sure to consider search engine optimisation (SEO) when coming up with your domain.

You want to communicate the type of business, be memorable, and not too long. Do you want to create an all-encompassing domain for your business or a domain name specific to your product? Australian domain names vary in pricing for two years.

Choosing Your Market and Developing Your Business Idea

People's most prominent struggle when starting any business is choosing a marketable idea that they enjoy doing. Unfortunately, there isn't an easy path to finding this perfect balance. Some soul searching is required to determine how you want to spend your day.

Sometimes the most marketable business won't make you happy in the long run. So instead, choose a business idea that you are excited about, are knowledgeable about and can see yourself doing five to ten years down the road.

Choosing a Niche Versus a Broad Market

Starting an online business requires some thought and planning. Before choosing which niche you want to go into or which market you want to pursue, there are many things to consider, and many people don't know where to start.

An excellent place to start is by thinking about what you enjoy doing or what skills you have that can be used in your business. Identifying your skills and interests will help you narrow down your target market.

There are advantages and disadvantages to both. There are two standard business models, where you either choose a niche or a broader (mass) market. In marketing, the term broad/mass markets and niche markets describe how general or specific are the group of people we aim to reach to sell our product or service.

A broad or mass market is very wide, meaning that you are targeting almost everyone, while a niche is narrow and represents a smaller group of people who all share distinctive characteristics.

If you are choosing a niche, it is better to be an expert in that specific area. For example, if you have expertise in pet care, you could start an e-commerce store specialising in pet products.

But if you are choosing to target a broader market, then try to be more of a generalist or provide something unique that the market doesn't have or that is hard to reproduce.

Choosing the Right Business Model

The most critical aspect of choosing a business model is the customer. To be profitable, you must provide a product or service people will want to buy.

The business model you choose should meet your target market's needs and fit your budget, production capacity and lifestyle. It's crucial to find a business idea that interests you over the long term, has a specific market or niche, and can provide a return on any investment.

Overview of Business Models to Consider

Which type of online business model is the best for your business? Selling a product isn't the only option. There are many types of companies that sell services instead of things. A service-based online business gives the owner even more flexibility and fewer overheads because they don't have to worry about inventory.

Take the time to consider the best online business model for your new idea, and you will dramatically increase your odds of success. Here are a few to consider:

- **E-commerce:** This is generally the model that comes to mind first when thinking of an online business. E-commerce is like having a digital retail store. You create or buy products, find a place to store the inventory, fulfil orders and promote your online store through various internet marketing strategies.

- **Affiliate marketing business:** This is where you push traffic to other people's e-commerce platforms and, in return, receive a commission.

- **Reselling business:** This could include buying and selling antiques, vintage clothes or even creating subscription boxes where you can curate an assortment of goods and package them into a single box to sell.

- **Drop-shipping:** This gives you the ability to create an e-commerce store and offer a wide range of products without stocking any inventory. When you make a sale, the factory ships the product to the customer.

  Drop-shipping is an ideal low-risk business model because it doesn't require investment in inventory or involve the costs associated with holding that stock. Plus, the supplier ships products for you, so you don't have to deal with the logistics related to that.

- **Digital services or online consulting:** You could offer a digital service that requires little to no overhead outside computer hardware, software and labour. Online businesses can provide social media management, blogging services, SEO services and paid advertising to other online companies.

  If you're a coach, mentor or expert in a specific field, another option could be to sell online consulting services. These business models are results-driven; you will have to show that you can bring value to a client before they pay for your service. While there are low overhead costs to start, convincing clients as a new company can be challenging.

Market Research and Idea Feasibility

Adequate market research can help new entrepreneurs decide what type of business is right for them. There are many ways to collect market research data, but how you do it depends on the type of information you need.

For example, surveys can be a great way to gather general information from many people. On the other hand, focus groups and interviews are better for gathering more experiential insights from just a few people.

Getting a feel for the market is crucial. You don't want to start a business that isn't viable; the only way to find out is to ask your target audience. You can undertake customer observation using a free SEO tool or a free trial of Semrush or Moz to check the search volume for your business idea.

If no one is googling your proposed business idea, you may want to go back to the drawing board.

Validating Your Idea

Once you have a couple of ideas that generate high-volume search engine results, you can test the interest by surveying people in your target audience. Some services will conduct surveys and market analysis for you, or you can use the power of the internet to see if your idea is viable via Facebook groups or other online communities where your target audience is accessible.

Survey Monkey is a great tool to effectively get a feel from a group of highly targeted potential customers. For a low fee per month, you can create an account and conduct fully customisable surveys.

Also, don't discount the opinion of friends and family. Ask anyone you respect about your business idea. Networking is an instrumental part of starting a business; you may be surprised by who shows an interest in your vision. Talking to as many people as possible could lead to business partners, clients or employees down the road.

Generating Revenue

Once you have developed a good understanding of the goals of your business and its target market, it will help you identify what products you want your online business to offer and how to price them.

Pricing Your Products or Services

Pricing your products is one of the most important decisions you'll need to make and will impact almost every aspect of your business. Your pricing is a deciding factor in everything from your cash flow to your profit margins to which expenses you can afford to cover.

Pricing your products and services can be a difficult decision. If you set your prices too high, your customers may find that your products are too expensive and turn to cheaper competitors. However, if you set your prices too low, it will affect your profits.

When you're pricing your products or services, it's important to consider:

- manufacturing cost
- your business's marketplace
- your competition
- market conditions

- brands
- quality of the product or service

Once you know the true cost of your product or service, you can then start analysing other influences and create your objectives and strategies.

If you're trying to find a price for your product, one easy method you can try is to add up all the fixed and variable costs involved in bringing your product to market and then add your profit margin on top of those expenses. However, just because it's the price you use to launch your business doesn't mean that it's the price you'll use forever.

When deciding your pricing strategy, the most critical objective is to ensure that your business is sustainable. If you price your products at a loss or an unsustainable profit margin, you're going to find it challenging to grow and scale.

Another aspect to consider when creating your pricing for an online product or service is your customer acquisition cost (CAC). New businesses struggle to have a realistic idea of how much it will cost them to generate traffic to the site. They don't know how many sales they will generate for every 100 visitors before going to market. The quality of your traffic and the cost of advertising all play a role in determining your CAC.

Be sure to take your time and thoroughly visualise every step in your business process and determine the cost along the way.

Defining Your Brand

What Is a Brand and Why Do You Need One?

Your brand is your company identity. Your choice of domain name, logo and styling needs to align with your business and products. One of the most important goals of branding is to differentiate your products or services from others in the market so that potential customers can easily recognise them.

The idea behind branding is to stand out from everyone else and make a statement about your company or yourself. However, a brand is also more than just a name. It is not just what you sell. It is how you do business, how you make decisions, and what you stand for. It's your business values and beliefs, and the one thing that sets your company apart from all the rest.

In a world where people are constantly looking for connections with their favourite brands, businesses must give their customers something they can relate to.

What Are Your Values and Differentiation?

In this age of digital opportunity, communicating your company values is a huge part of doing business. Well-defined core brand values are the beliefs that you as a company stand for. They are essential in guiding your brand story, actions, behaviours and decision-making process.

Why does your brand exist, and why should consumers care? What will success look like for your brand? What are the fundamental values that your brand will embody?

These days, people are much more conscious when shopping for products. As a result, many customers want to support businesses whose brand values make a meaningful impact in some way, whether it's by using ethical materials or sustainable packaging or by that business providing a product or service that is unique and meaningful. Your brand purpose will be the core of everything that you do after that.

As well as being a freelance web designer and e-commerce specialist, I am one of the founders of Spend with Us – Buy

From a Bush Business (https://www.spendwithus.com.au), an online marketplace and community that support rural and regional Australian small businesses to sell their products online. It's a great brand to use as an example in this section to highlight an effective brand value proposition.

Our customers know that when they shop with us, they are making a difference to hundreds of small bush businesses across Australia, of which bushfires, drought and the pandemic have impacted. We make this clear across all our branding, website and social media posts that consumers make a difference when they shop on Spend With Us.

How can you make your brand and business stand out from the competition? Your brand values and purpose should clarify why customers should buy from your business rather than your competitor.

Creating Your Online Presence

What Technology Do You Need to Start Your Online Business?

Once you have done market research and defined your brand, it's time to create your online presence. If you're comfortable with technology, building a DIY website can be easily achieved using an abundance of free or inexpensive platforms and resources readily available online.

However, it can be overwhelming for less tech-savvy individuals because there are *so many* options, and it's difficult to know where to start. In this section, I'll go through some of the fundamental technology platforms you can use to get started as a small business commencing its online journey.

Creating your own website store or page where customers can go to and directly purchase your products or services via online payment is essential for an online business.

A Facebook page or Instagram account is acceptable as a starting point. Still, customers cannot yet checkout directly using these platforms in Australia. This means that you will be losing out on sales from customers who can't be bothered to message back and forth to organise payment and want to make the purchase right there and then.

These days, consumers expect more. If you don't have a web address to direct people to or a way to take payment directly online, your online business doesn't look professional and won't be taken seriously.

Suppose you are only selling your products via social media. In that case, you are entirely at the mercy of the social media network's algorithm, and that is not a solid foundation on which to build your business.

We will look at three approaches you can use to start selling online.

**Option 1 –
Build your website on a self-hosted platform:**

A self-hosted platform involves purchasing a web hosting service and creating your website using a content management system (CMS) such as WordPress or Magento. The running expenses will be lower, you will have complete control over the website features and functionality, but the development and maintenance costs will be higher.

If you don't have any technical knowledge or sufficient time to create something that will look professional, it's easy to find a specialist to hire to help you. There are also hundreds if not thousands of tutorials and courses available on YouTube, Udemy, Lynda and SkillShare to learn more about CMS.

Or you can decide to outsource the entire process and work with a digital agency or freelancer to design and develop your site for you. As a freelance web designer myself, I know all too well how much time and skill goes into creating a professional, responsive, user-friendly, and SEO optimised website that is easy to drive traffic to. Hiring a professional is always my recommendation if you have the budget.

Option 2 –
Use a managed e-commerce platform:

You'll need to pay a monthly fee to use platforms such as Shopify, Wix or Squarespace, but no code or knowledge of computer science is required. Instead, you simply follow instructions and can create an e-commerce store with a secure payment gateway. You can also seek the guidance of a web designer who specialises in these platforms for a smooth and professional implementation.

Option 3 –
Create your online presence using an existing online marketplace:

You can consider creating your online presence using an online marketplace that already has an existing customer base of people who want to purchase your products or services.

For example, if you are a small, rural business, you could create an online store on Spend With Us. The marketplace has a ready and waiting audience and community of over 330,000 members looking to purchase products from Australian rural and regional small businesses.

Another example, if you sell handmade products, you could create an Etsy store and access their user base of customers looking to discover and buy handmade products. The benefits of using a marketplace to sell your products are plenty.

In addition, most marketplaces are low cost or even free to start selling! You can set up an e-commerce store instantly, and no coding is necessary.

Marketplaces can also help you get new customers! People who have never heard of your website, products or services will find you. The marketplace does all the website maintenance, SEO, social media and Google ads to drive traffic to your store, so you don't have to.

Online marketplaces can assist your business to gain trust and reputability. They can help a small business that is starting out to gain quality brand awareness and recognition.

Each of these options can give you a solid online business presence. Which one you choose depends on your level of comfort with technology and the time you have available to launch your online business.

Many small businesses create their own website *and* sell through an online marketplace as inventory, product listings and orders can synchronise between platforms with the correct setup. The more your business, brand and products are getting seen, the more sales you will achieve!

This brings us onto our next and final section to start your online business …

Getting Traffic to Your Website

It's great to have a beautiful website, but if no one knows it exists, you won't be making many sales. So, the first step is to find out where your target audience hangs out.

What's their preferred online space?

Which social networking sites do they use the most?

What channels will make them open your emails?

Once you answer these questions, you can build your targeted audience and attract them to your website.

Getting visitors to your website (or any online destination you want consumers to purchase from) is often one of the most challenging parts of launching an online business. Still, once you get through this stage, everything will be much easier.

Where Will You Find Your Target Audience?

Finding your audience takes time, trial and error. The beauty of digital advertising is that you have data to discover what is working and what isn't.

One way to get an idea of where your audience could be is by looking at the competition to get an idea of what is working for them:

- Do they have social media? How active are they?
- Are they running social media ads?
- Do you start to see retargeting ads after clicking on their website?
- Do they run any traditional advertising (TV, radio, newspaper)?
- Are they using their blog? How many posts per month?
- Do they have an email marketing list and strategy?
- Where do they show up on search results?

Once you understand what competitive businesses are doing for advertising, it will be easier to develop your own marketing strategy.

You want to aim for high-quality website traffic. The calibre of the traffic to your site is significantly more important than volume. It's essential to understand your ideal customer because you want to drive quality traffic to your website.

Quality website traffic is visitors to your site that are genuinely interested in the product or service you are providing. These people are your target audience.

Generating traffic will be one of the biggest challenges. Moving up the Google search rankings and building a loyal social media following are long-term strategies. In the beginning, you will most likely be frustrated, and everything will seem hopeless, but if you stick to a solid digital marketing strategy, you will see results.

The best way to know whether traffic to your site is valuable is to set up event, goal or e-commerce tracking within your Google Analytics account. If this all sounds too daunting, there are many SEO, Google and social media ad specialists who can help you set these things up and know what to look for.

New businesses tend to struggle to have a realistic idea of how much it will cost them to generate traffic to the site. They don't know how many sales they will generate for every 100 visitors before going to market. The quality of your traffic and the cost of advertising all play a role in determining your CAC.

Let's look at the three most important traffic sources you should use to drive consumers to your online business.

Search Engine Optimisation

SEO is complicated. As internet search technology grows and improves, it becomes harder and harder to rank in the top ten to fifty search engine results for any keyword. Therefore, the importance of choosing SEO keywords with lower competition has increased dramatically.

It takes a mixture of blogging, optimising pages for keywords, inbound, outbound and backlinks. No matter which platform you have used to set up your online store, effective SEO marketing is essential for driving quality traffic towards a site. SEO is a long-term process, and you generally can't get the best out of it until you optimise the entire content of an online store.

To get the best out of SEO, I always suggest hiring an expert. If you are looking to save some money, though, you can do many online courses to learn the basics and try them out yourself. SEO isn't technically challenging; you just have to know what you are doing.

Social Media

It's easy to feel overwhelmed by social media; just remember that you don't need to have a presence on every single platform out there. Instead, choose the social media platforms that are the most relevant to your audience, your brand proposition and the nature of your product or service. Generally, Facebook and Instagram should be the primary platforms you start with, simply because most people use them.

Facebook is much more than just a place to connect with friends – it's also an excellent marketing toolkit. You can use it to upload videos, pictures or media and create ads with different functions, such as driving site traffic.

Email Marketing

Leveraging effective email marketing is one of the most convenient and straightforward ways to drive traffic to your online business. As one of the most traditional web marketing forms, email campaigns can help you generate organic traffic.

In addition, by taking advantage of email, you can keep in touch with your customers and encourage them to make future purchases. You'll even boost second-purchase conversions. Having customers come back regularly is critically important for any business as it has a significant impact on their CAC.

Conclusion

There has never been a more exciting or accessible time for people to start an online small business. This chapter has discussed the main concepts to plan and consider when starting an online business. These include validating and choosing your product or service to sell, researching your target audience, how to price your products and services, developing your brand, choosing an online platform to sell from and ways to drive traffic to that platform.

There is so much more that we could delve into, but the most critical part of starting an online business is to take action! You can start building your online business and creating strategies to put in place all while still working at your regular job if you have one.

Persist and don't give up is my advice. There are likely to be many times when you want to quit and forget it all, but don't! A successful online business does not happen overnight.

You will need to keep on learning and improving. But if you keep at it and put in the hard work, have faith that your business will succeed, and you will have achieved something that you can be very proud of. You will be glad that you never gave up.

About the Author

Sarah Britz is a Web Designer and Developer specialising in e-commerce for small businesses. She is also the co-Founder of Spend With Us – Buy From a Bush Business, an online shopping marketplace and community supporting hundreds of Australian rural and regional small businesses to sell online. She has worked in the digital media space for over 20 years and has a broad range of industry experience in design, inception and development.

Sarah has a strong passion for helping businesses and individuals fulfil their dreams and bring their ideas to digital life. She specialises in designing websites that stand out, make an impact and get results!

Growing up in the UK, Sarah spent most of her late teens and twenties travelling and working around the world. She and her husband, Andy, emigrated to Australia in 2013. They live on a rural property on the beautiful Central Coast, NSW, the perfect place for their two young children to grow up.

Sarah created Spend With Us, the first e-commerce platform that exclusively services rural and regional communities, focusing on supporting businesses impacted by bushfires and drought. During the 2019/20 bushfires, she realised that many small businesses in rural bushfire affected areas had no online presence to keep trading, sell their products, and earn an income when they couldn't get to markets, or their bricks and mortar stores were closed. Spend With Us helped connect these bush businesses with the city and bring money back into these communities that had seen no tourism come through for months.

After the bushfires and drought came COVID-19, which impacted even more small businesses. Sarah continues to support bushfire, drought, and coronavirus impacted rural and regional Australian small businesses through her work with Spend With Us. In addition, she offers responsive website design and development services via her digital design consultancy to small businesses across Australia and the globe.

Sarah Britz

Website: https://www.sarahbritz.com.au/

Facebook: https://www.facebook.com/britzdigitaldesign/

LinkedIn: https://www.linkedin.com/in/sarahbritz/

Spend With Us

Website: https://www.spendwithus.com.au/

Chapter Seven
Finding the Gaps in the Market
(And What Sets You Apart)

By Lisa Woods
Wimmera Wellness

The Beginning

Here I sit, it's approximately ten o'clock in the morning and I'm joined in warmth by my second cup of coffee for the day. At the moment, my baby is currently asleep, so I'm just taking a little time out for myself procaffeinating and taking a quick scroll through the socials.

Everything is fine until once again I am confronted by a Facebook business post asking the same question, sharing the same conundrum. I find that time after time I get more frustrated because I'm seeing it over and over again, and I wonder why people are not learning these lessons. How do they not know this before they go into business?

My story of going into business is perhaps the same as yours, or maybe it's not at all. You see, five and a half years ago my first child was born. As the story goes, he was such a good sleeper. One of my friends who I used to work with suggested that I take a short course.

What would somebody who is university qualified possibly study as a short course, I asked myself. I didn't mean to sound arrogant. I was genuinely curious. I thought that studying six years at university and a number of other courses meant that I was at capacity in my learning – apparently not.

She gently said to me, "I know you've been loving your essential oils, why don't you delve a little deeper?"

Because I had a three-hour block of time every afternoon, I thought, let's do it. I was so hungry to learn that I breezed through the course and graduated at the top of my class. I graduated with a distinction in a diploma of Aromatherapy.

I was hooked! I wanted to learn more and more about this natural approach where I could support my family and our health, physically and emotionally. It was a change from the legal textbooks that I was used to pouring over. This was literally breathing life into me!

Born out of the need of conditions or concerns that my own family was facing was my business Wimmera Wellness. But that's way too quick, isn't it? Let me slow down and tell you how it went.

As I learnt about the oils, I needed to complete assignments. I compiled recipes and made products that I gave to friends and family to try. I knew I was onto something when they would finish using a product that I had created for an assessment, and they would ask me to make it again because, in their words, "It works!"

Bringing a Solution to a Pain Point

To begin with I was a little shocked I thought we only bought products for babies' skin and health from the pharmacy or the supermarket like this. I didn't realise that there was this whole world out there where I could create products myself that are all natural, have actual benefits, and work!

Word soon spread among my friends and family, and then their friends and family were contacting me asking for a blend for one reason or another. At this point in time, I realised that I needed to get some insurance to cover myself and maybe even come up with a business name, because maybe this little hobby of mine could earn me some money on the side.

I went with the name Wimmera Wellness, because the Wimmera is the region that we live in, and wellness, well, I guess that's self-explanatory. In hindsight, had I known how big my business would get, I may have chosen a different name, or I may not have?

The name is now synonymous not just in my region but around the state and indeed Australia as a brand of choice and trust for natural skin products.

This business of mine was born out of need, out of the pain that either myself or somebody else was feeling that I was able to bring a solution to. If you're following along and taking notes, the **first** thing I would love for you to remember is when you were looking at going into business **what is the pain point that you can create a solution for?**

I see too many well-meaning people going about setting up businesses and doing something they think will earn them a lot of money, only to realise heartache and disappointment at the end of the day. Why? Because there was neither a need for their product on the market nor a pain point that they were solving.

You might be wondering what was on the Facebook business post that I was talking about at the beginning of my chapter. It was basically what I have just covered here. People said that they have gone and purchased all these stocks and set up a business but could not generate any sales.

Straight away my first thought is what was the pain point that they were solving? With clothing shops on every corner and indeed so many more online, what were they thinking that would set them apart from the rest?

Now you may be reading this and think, I want to start a clothing range or I want to open a clothing shop – I'm not telling you not to. What I'm simply saying is what is the pain point that you are a bringing solution to?

I can think of a couple of businesses in the wider Wimmera region where I live that have done this exceptionally well. A businessowner has opened a clothing boutique in a very small country town and is experiencing great success both online and in-store sales.

One might look and say how was that even possible when large discount chain stores are just half an hour away, but the answer is that she has found a pain point and brought a solution to it.

Just because we live in the country doesn't mean that we don't follow clothing or fashion trends, and it doesn't mean that we don't want to look our best.

The owner of this business has brought the best of what the city and our urban cousins have to offer and has brought it to the country in a bright, colourful and bubbly way and is really succeeding. She also has other tips and tricks at her disposal, which makes her stand out, and I applaud her for that!

In the same way I would caution that just because you are in a population-dense area doesn't mean you have an automatic right to have sales and make money. Unless you are meeting a pain point with a solution, you will find it difficult to succeed.

Your friends and family may purchase from you in the beginning, but even after a while they will exhaust their funds.

Getting the Right Qualifications

Once you have established what the pain point is that you want to solve, you need to ask yourself if there are any qualifications involved.

Let me give you the 411 on my industry. I have seen so many people peddling essential oil blends that they put together and sell them on online platforms. Not only is the price not reflective, but I also have to ask if they have any qualifications in putting these blends together.

To the best of my knowledge there are only two or three of us around the area at the moment who are qualified to make and sell the blends that we produce. Not only are we qualified, but we have the appropriate insurance to cover ourselves.

Knowledge is powerful – knowledge of the product, knowledge of contra indications and knowledge of what your consumer needs.

Although you might say to me that you are just working from home, surely you don't need insurance because you are not renting a building and you don't have a shopfront. Unfortunately, you do.

My business insurance is comprehensive and drills right down to the relevant information and qualifications that I have to produce my products.

If you're still following along and taking notes, the second thing I want you to ask yourself is, **"What relevant qualifications or insurance do I need?"**

Growing Your Business

Once you've worked those things out then it's time to get to work. **Grow a solid social media following,** even if you don't have anything to sell just yet.

Go on a big hunt through the internet, save a heap of photos, post them to your socials (obviously giving credit to where you have seen them) and attract people towards your website landing page so that when you launch a new product you already have somebody to launch it to.

Of course, I'm not talking about just any photos but photos of things that inspire you, the same colour theme, quotes and the like. Just because you don't yet have anything to sell, doesn't mean you don't yet have anything to say.

Another one of my pet hates is when I'm doing my 10 am scroll and I see another person say that they're so frustrated of not getting any sales. When I comment and ask them about their social media following, they say that it's really not that great, and so my immediate question is, "Well, who are these people who know that you're in business, and why would they buy from you if they don't know you exist?"

The owner of the clothing shop I mentioned earlier, I don't even know if she has a qualification in fashion, but I feel as though she knows more than me about fashion. I looked at her and I realised that if she's wearing a dress a certain way and she's pairing it with a set of earrings that I like and maybe even a lipstick, I'm tempted to buy the whole combination from her because I see it on her, and frankly, I want it.

She showed me time and again through her social media the use of colour, pattern and style. I subscribe to it and I like it, and thus I want to buy it. She makes purchasing from her shop really simple, and it's a nice, clean process.

I remember in the early days before I had a website, I would generate most of my sales from word-of-mouth or at a market. Indeed, that was how I built my business in the early days. Now with three children afoot, I don't have the time to go to weekend markets, but I also don't need to do this anymore because my business has enough credit and enough wholesalers now that it's in a self-propelling motion.

Can we just talk about that for a moment? I am what society refers to as a stay-at-home mum. My husband goes out to *work* and I am home as the primary caregiver to our three sons.

I always said that I would build this business around my babies, so as a rule of thumb I try to avoid any work while they are around and I generally do most of it during their nap time, or after seven o'clock at night when they are asleep.

In the early days I had to do a lot of this, but now it's evened out and I have a good strategy in place. Do I have it all together? Absolutely not! But I have worked out some simple processes and what I want from my business. Implementing those boundaries means that I know how and when I can operate, and I feel safe with that.

Just because you are a stay-at-home mum does not mean that you cannot build a successful six-figure business, or even a successful five-figure hobby on the side. It's important to ask yourself every year, **what do I want for my business, how can my business serve my family, and how can I make it work?**

Set aside time to think and plan.

In my business I find that it's really useful to have mini launches when I am launching a new collection or a new product. In the early days, I used to just whack it on my website and blindly hope that people would find it and purchase from me. You know, sometimes they did, but most of the times they didn't.

So, the strategy that I love the most is to give sneak peaks to my followers. Using the arsenal of tools available on social media, especially Instagram, in the week leading up to a launch, I love to have sneak peaks, polls, quizzes, message boxes, pumping music and all the while pushing people towards my mailing list.

Remember, I said that you need to have somebody to launch your product to, these are some of the successful strategies that you can use to help boost a product launch.

I have also found social media to be the number one place for me to build and promote my business. As my business name really is me, I know that my followers love to see my face.

Recently, I've really enjoyed using reels on Instagram, and even though they may not be the punchiest ones made by an acting or dance professional, they are effective and they get my message across.

I've also found recently that getting back into my love of dance has been quite good for my mental health and so it's a win-win for my business and me personally.

However, not everything in business is easy …

The Pivot

At the beginning of 2021, I thought the Covid-19 crisis would be behind us, and so I grabbed my vision board and wrote my big plans for this year. It wasn't long into it that we got back on the Covid-coaster of lockdown after lockdown. My wholesalers were not ordering as much as usual because their retail spaces were not open to customers.

I had to pivot. I started aggressively promoting my products to my social media community again so that sales would pick up. It worked.

But I also had a brilliant idea – white label. I don't really know how it came about to be honest, all I can think of was that during my son's newborn phase, I must've had a crazy idea during a 3 am feed. Here we are and it's working!

I approached some of my existing retailers to see if they would like for me to create a product under their name and branding to sell online or in their retail store. I wasn't expecting so many of them to agree, so initially I was swamped! But that's a great problem to have in small businesses, isn't it?

My baby boy turned one this year. Living during a pandemic, it's a sad realisation that he has lived all of his life on a Covid-coaster and much of it in lockdown. I'll be damned if that's what he thinks of his formative years. I am doing all in my power to make life "normal", fun and positive.

I continue to be a work-from-home mum. I drop my eldest to school when he's not remote learning, we head to the post office to collect parcels and deposit orders for shipping.

I always grab my coffee before we head home for playtime and morning tea. My favourite is building blocks. Samuel loves to give himself a clap when he makes a stack. It's adorable. When naptime rolls around (thankfully, it's two and a half hours long) I make my coffee, roll up my sleeves and get to work.

There's always a human wearing a million hats behind any small business, right? I'm Lisa, and if you strip away all the labels, I make products I'd buy myself because I know exactly what goes into them (and what doesn't).

As a certified aromatherapist, I have the professional training and skills to make them with full integrity. I stand by every single product in the range because they were created for my family. There's no way I will compromise their health with chemical-laden, mass-produced products loosely promoted as skincare.

I love essential oils, coffee (I'm a mum of three boys under five and run a business – coffee is life), all things leopard print and my family.

Wimmera Wellness grew from my love of helping people, and from being begged to make my special formulas for friends and their friends, and the word grew so quickly that it became an Australia-wide online business that retains its personal care.

I'm still a mum living in regional Australia, who cares about every product I share with others.

Stay well and remember, there is an oil for that!

About the Author

Lisa Woods is the health driven founder and creator of Wimmera Wellness, an Australian-based online aromatherapies specialist business. As a passionate advocate for health and wellbeing, she is a highly qualified and experienced aromatherapist who loves essential oils and helping people to pursue their wellness journey.

Wimmera Wellness was born from her personal mission to find solutions for health conditions and concerns which impacted her family. It was also born from her goal to find and utilise natural products, over pharmacy products and mass production. With an innovative drive, Lisa set out to discover how wonderfully supportive nature really is to our health and fell deeply in love with essential oils.

To educate herself and understand the fundamentals of her future direction and goals, she pursued a Diploma of Aromatherapy and with excellence graduated with a distinction.

The result of her efforts was to create a unique health business which supported her family and provided wonderful physical and emotional results. Using her knowledge, she compiled unique recipes and made products which her family and friends adored. From this positive response she knew she was onto an amazing collection of natural products which worked! With a high level of integrity and a genuine care for people, she now produces high quality aromatherapy products which are personalised, consciously made and dedicated to her clients' needs.

Happily married to Dion and mother of three gorgeous boys; Joshua, Jonathan and Samuel, Lisa is a family woman who successfully juggles motherhood, being a loving wife and the exciting lifestyle of entrepreneurship. Living in regional Victoria close to the beautiful Richardson River, Lisa also finds her solace in supporting other women in business because she understands the importance of empowerment and the journey and challenges of entrepreneurship.

"I'm incredibly grateful for every single person who has supported my rural Australian business over the corporations who prioritise profits over people and don't give back local communities. From the bottom of my heart, thank you."

Stay well and remember, there is an oil for that ;)

Lisa

Website: https://wimmerawellness.com.au/

Facebook: https://www.facebook.com/wimmerawellness/

Instagram: https://www.instagram.com/wimmerawellness/

Chapter Eight

The Value of Education for Women:
An Opportunity to Poverty-Proof Your Future

By Gillian Hehir
Victoria Street Psychology

Introduction

"You always fall on your feet," said my mother many years ago. It struck me then that it wasn't luck or fate, it was my strong will, steely determination and perseverance that got me back on my feet.

I grabbed opportunities that came my way and created them when I couldn't find them. I only ever looked back to learn from my own life experiences, but my approach to life was always forward thinking and forward planning. If things weren't working, I changed direction.

From Humble Beginnings

I was born in the early sixties into a farming family in rural New South Wales. The nearest town and school were about thirty kilometres away. I travelled that road for many years on the school bus and in the family car.

I was the youngest and only daughter in my family, with four older brothers. My father, having survived as a prisoner of war during the Second World War, was granted a Soldier Settlement block of around 1,500 acres. This is where we all grew up.

Life on the farm was simple, mostly self-sufficient and idyllic for me: a shy young girl who loved the outdoors and, in particular, horses.

My mother had trained as a nurse and midwife. Unfortunately, she had no opportunities to return to the career she loves so much. She and Dad were pioneers in a somewhat remote and harsh environment, particularly in the early years, where it was often a daily struggle for survival.

With mutual support from neighbouring families, Mum and Dad managed to build fences, dams, homes and, in time, a family.

My local small-town schooling gave me little ambition. Being "smart" seemed to be what boys did, but not girls. In my mind, young women grew up, married a local farmer and had children. I knew no other life and there were no other women around me who worked beyond bringing up their families and helping out on the farm.

I had a great aunt, who I am named after. She worked and travelled the world, sending me postcards and bringing back little trinkets from far-off and exotic places, so perhaps somewhere in there, I thought there could be more to life.

An Opportunity to Witness the Value of Education

I will be forever grateful that, somewhere in my early years, my parents recognised that I was smart and many years later my mother remarked that she'd felt I would never have been happy settling for the life she had.

I was given the opportunity to attend boarding school at the age of fourteen. I agreed to go only if I could take my horse and my best friend could come too (and her horse!) – so off we went to boarding school.

It was a school with a fine academic reputation, and I had opportunities there I could never have experienced at my local country high school. I also saw other women, both fellow students and teachers, who were ambitious and valued education.

I started to recognise what I could be capable of and, for the first time in my life, realised it was alright to be smart, female and to have dreams beyond being a wife and mother.

Living the High Life Until ...

When I finished secondary school, I couldn't wait to move down to Melbourne. I had outgrown my small country town and the bright lights of the big city beckoned. So off we ventured, my best friend and me, to The Big Smoke.

Although still feeling like a very young and naïve little country girl, I eventually embraced life in Melbourne. Following a couple of years of business studies at RMIT, I threw myself, with lots of enthusiasm, into work in the film industry, television, advertising and other media.

My "business studies" course was really secretarial school. Although I loved my work, I initially still felt a bit like I was filling in time until I met the man of my dreams, married and became a mother. My course would still lead to very traditional roles for women: secretaries, nurses and teachers.

Being ambitious to have my own career and support myself financially during the "affluent eighties", was still just something I dreamed about but never fully accepted as something that I could achieve.

I loved working, particularly in the fields I chose, and seemed to do well because somewhere in there, the shy young girl from the country grew into a quietly confident young woman and was actually very good with people and endlessly curious about the human psyche.

I soon moved beyond the secretarial roles and worked in account service, sales and marketing.

I also travelled the world during this time for work and pleasure, and became an avid snow-skier, much to the concern of my family. Life was great!

Then I met a man who I believed at the time was the man of my dreams. Following a whirlwind romance, we married, set up home together and I found myself pregnant at the age of thirty-two.

By thirty-three, I was a struggling sole parent with a three-month-old son. I returned to work and put my beautiful little boy into full-time childcare in Melbourne. Somehow, it just didn't feel right.

I again remembered my mother saying, "You always fall on your feet", as well as being extremely determined when I put my mind to something. I had to find a way to get back on my feet and to build a future for myself and my young son. He was all the motivation I needed.

Back to School to Support Myself and My Son

So back I went to university. First with a fine arts degree, as I'd always loved art, then onto a psychology degree and eventually a master's in clinical psychology. This all took around 11 years of juggling study, work placements, voluntary work, paid work and bringing up my son.

Somewhere along the way, at the age of forty, I even managed to buy my own home, with the encouragement of the local female bank manager who seemed to see my potential.

Having been rejected, as a sole parent, part-time worker and full-time university student, by the major banks, I then approached the local credit union and met with the manager. Her words to me were, "In my experience, sole parents do all they can to keep a roof over their heads." She approved my first mortgage and I didn't look back.

At the age of forty-eight, I qualified as a psychologist and began work at the local private hospital two days a week. I also set up my own private practice, eventually recognising that I really wanted to find my niche.

My niche, for a number of reason and life experiences, meant working exclusively with women. This is where I built my practice with the work I love.

Living My Potential and Helping Other Women Reach Theirs

I remember having a party at home in late 2008 to celebrate my achievements. I had recently sold my first home, purchased my second, qualified as a psychologist and was working hard in both my private practice and at the hospital.

My sixteen-year-old son was happy and sociable, doing reasonably well at school and was growing into a delightful young man, despite having no contact with his father for many years. Life, again, was good!

To my amazement, life just got better. In the following year, I met my future husband. He really was, and still is, the man of my dreams and my life partner. Life felt complete when we eventually married and moved into our beautiful patch of paradise on the edge of Ballarat three years later.

Somewhere along the way, however, I felt that I needed a new project. I tossed around three ideas: go back to university and do my PhD, write a book called "Why Women Worry" based on my work, or set up my own private practice in my own building.

I yearned to have my own consulting space where I could surround myself with beautiful things and with like-minded people passionate about making a difference in our small part of the world through psychology.

With my husband's blessing and support, I purchased a beautiful old Victorian home in Victoria Street in Ballarat. Then I set about converting it into a commercial property, with four consulting rooms to relocate my own private practice and to hand-pick colleagues to share the remaining rooms.

What I anticipated to be a relatively easy and seamless process took two years of roadblocks, bureaucracy and determination. But with the support of my husband, my son, my family and various experts, including a wonderful builder I met along the way, Victoria Street Psychology came to fruition and was launched in November 2018.

Since then, I have been able to offer rooms to a number of other remarkably talented female psychologists who have been busy building their own independent private practices within our beautiful building. Life is still good!

What I've Learnt

- Find what you believe you are really good at and look at ways of making a living out of it.
- If you need further study, do your homework, find what you need to do and make a whole-hearted commitment to follow it through.
- It's not the brightest and smartest who succeed

with further study at a tertiary level, it's those who stick with it and persevere, with one eye always on the end goal.

- There are no right or wrong decisions. They are purely choices we make at the time based on what we know and understand at that point. Once made, try to make it work. If it's not working, take another path.

- There are **always** options – even if those options don't seem very appealing.

- Surround yourself with people who support your goals.

- If you're feeling "stuck" or lacking direction at any point in your life, consider talking to a psychologist or therapist. Psychologists don't just work with people who have mental health issues.

  Among other things, they help individuals sort through their own internal mind, inner dialogue, and explore behaviours that may be getting in their way and help find a way forward. A psychologist can also offer a non-biased and non-judgemental perspective on your life that trusted friends and family may struggle with.

- Biology gives us a brain; life gives us a mind. It's worth trying to understand and appreciate your unique "way of being" in the world and whether you have deep-seated core beliefs about yourself that may be getting in the way. A therapist can help you sort through your mind and understand yourself more effectively.

- Be willing to take risks … just make sure that you do your homework and that they are calculated risks.

- Find good professional support around you to outsource the things that you're not necessarily expert at.

- Find ways to look after yourself physically, mentally and emotionally including prioritising good-quality sleep. It's the very foundation of our well-being. Running on empty will just continue to deplete you. Good sleep and keeping physically well gives you a "buffer zone" for when things don't go according to plan. Chances are things won't go according to plan.

- Plan but always learn to be flexible.

- As a woman, financial independence is definitely worth working towards for the choices and options it will give you.

- As humans, we are emotional beings. It's ok to feel emotions. Even the ones we may not necessarily like, such as anger. Anger is energy. Use it wisely and it can serve you well.

- Understand the difference between "helpful thinking" and "unhelpful thinking". If there is something to worry about, the human mind will find it and ruminate about it. If it's not serving you well, try and let it go and focus on problem-solving where you can.

- As humans, we are natural problem-solvers and more resilient than we realise.

Conclusion

My work with women over the years, in my practice has taught me a number of things. The things I recognise most, however, are the "stuck feelings", particularly for women who may want to leave an unhappy relationship but who feel reliant on the other person to survive financially.

This often forces them to make compromises that they are not comfortable with.

They often feel powerless to achieve any sort of financial security or independence and find themselves without a way to make a living. The answer often involves further study.

Another thing I notice is that women become immobilised around decision-making for fear of making the wrong decision. I have realised during my life that there are no wrong decisions but there are simply the choices we make at the time based on what we know and understand in that moment.

Once we've made those choices, we need to try our hardest to make them work. If things are not working in a way we'd hoped, we need to reconsider our choices and move in another direction.

Knowledge is power and education is part of that knowledge. Know what you're good at and pursue it sooner rather than later.

Don't give up.

As a woman, I am grateful for the opportunities I had to enable me to achieve what I have through educating myself.

It's never too late to start.

About the Author

Gillian Hehir MAPS FCCLP

Clinical Psychologist

BA Hons(Psych) MPsych(Clin)

Gillian Hehir is a clinical psychologist working in private practice in Ballarat. She is passionate about the well-being of women and works exclusively with those who identify as female. Gillian is a proud feminist and much of her work involves assisting women to recognise the value of financial and emotional independence to ensure their individual choices and options in life.

Gillian undertook all her tertiary studies and associated work placements in Ballarat and retains a strong connection to the university and local health professionals. She continues to supervise and mentor trainee psychologists to pass on her experience and wisdom to ensure the capacity and sustainability of the next generation of fellow health professionals, in what can be a very rewarding but also often challenging, career path.

When not working, Gillian enjoys the peace and tranquillity of a 5-acre property on the outskirts of Ballarat which she shares with her husband, two cats and various other animals and wildlife. She enjoys tending the garden, reading, cooking, hiking, keeping fit and spending time with friends and family and, as a creative pursuit, she has developed a keen interest in the art of mosaic.

Gillian remains immensely proud of her son, now twenty-seven, as he forges his way in the world, which currently includes a return to study in the pursuit of his passion to make a difference in his small part of the world.

For further information see: www.gillianhehir.com.au

Chapter Nine
Bootstrapping Your Business

By Anna Barwick
PharmOnline

Introduction

Bootstrapping is building a business or company from the ground up with nothing but personal savings and cash coming in from the first sales. It includes the use of personal income, taking on personal debt or borrowing from friends and family.

Often, the founder/s continue to work in another job and begin this new business as a side hustle. If this is you, you are not alone. Welcome to entrepreneurship!

More than three quarters of start-ups primarily fund themselves this way.

The median start-up funding is around $10,000. To start a business and bring it to successful fruition requires confidence, risk tolerance, self-discipline, determination and competitiveness.

You will develop a wide variety of skills to be resourceful and resilient.

There are pros and cons to bootstrapping. It means that you have total control over business decisions and where money is spent. Bootstrapping allows entrepreneurs to experiment with their product offering and slowly build revenue that can fund future investments.

Bootstrapped businesses expect to be around for a long time, growing slowly and expanding their paying customer base to meet the business costs.

However, it also means that all financial risk is on you. Limited resources can affect the potential for growth and scaling or even undermine the quality of your product or service.

Many businesses start this way until they can raise venture capital or other outside funding. There are some amazing companies that were bootstrapped into multimillion-dollar companies including Facebook, Spanx and Tough Mudder.

Here are some tips that can help you in those early days and stages of your business if bootstrapping is the way to go.

Set Your Budget

Outlining your income and expenditure over a specific period will allow you to plan how to effectively use the money you have. Estimating sales can give you an idea of a breakeven point – the time when your spending is matched by the money you are bringing in.

This can often take months or even years, so it is important to identify when you can afford to spend more or when you need to reconsider if your business costs are serving you well.

Be aware that investing in some areas, such as outsourced public relations and marketing, can be very costly and may not offer a good return. Initially, you may have to do much of this yourself, using low-cost methods including social media posts, pitching writing pieces to publications that target your ideal customer or speaking on podcasts to promote your business.

A separate bank account for your business is highly recommended so you can see all the money going in and out. This helps you to balance your accounting as you go.

Love Your Spreadsheet

Using an online spreadsheet allows you to keep track of expenses and income. Although you may prefer writing this out by hand, it is essential to have an electronic form that can be easily manipulated and adjusted as numbers change.

Your spreadsheet can be as simple as an Excel or Numbers sheet or on a specialised accounting software programme such as Xero or QuickBooks Online to keep track.

All entries should be separate from your personal expenses to make tax time and Business Activity Statements (BAS) easier to manage. You can generate a balance sheet, cashflow or profit and loss (income) statements and these can be incorporated into your broader business plan.

Knowing how to do these can be tricky but there are always YouTube videos that you can watch to help you upskill for free.

Check In Regularly

It is important to invest in growth areas of your business. You need to monitor this, for example monthly, so that you can re-route funding where it is needed while still sticking to your budget. Never over-commit yourself financially as it will cause you stress and may result in missed business opportunities.

Setting a time point for reassessing your financial inputs into your new business is critical; you can't keep sinking money into something with no financial return when you are bootstrapping.

Get Financial Advice

A financial advisor can provide insight for planning ahead, particularly around superannuation. You may have been looking after your own taxes up until this point but an accountant with small business expertise is equipped to find tax breaks for you and grants that you may be eligible for.

You need an accountant that explains what they are doing and why so that you can understand the value they bring to your business. Keep in close contact with these experts, as they can save you money and make your money work harder. Remember that you will need to keep track of all of your expenses and income, so keep all receipts and invoices for tax time.

Ask For a Payment Plan

To help you stick to your budget, it means outlining the weekly, fortnightly, monthly or yearly costs you need to pay. You may get a significant discount by signing up to a service, such as a social media management platform, by paying yearly; however, this may not suit your cash-flow needs.

Break Up Your Spend

Paying your costs fortnightly or monthly may work better when you are bootstrapping, even if it costs slightly more in the long run

 If you know that you get a regular income from another job that is paid fortnightly, you can set up an automatic payment from your account as soon as it is deposited, to pay off your bills. You can select a plan in a subscription or contract so that it is timed with when you can afford to pay it.

Push Payments Back Where Possible

All you need to do is ask! Other businesses understand the financial pressures associated with gaining customers, so it is worthwhile asking to delay payments if you can't afford them right now. This includes your phone and internet bills; many large corporations will set up payment plans that may help you as well.

It only becomes a problem if you are not communicating with the businesses where you owe money. I have always been pleasantly surprised when I've asked to have payments pushed back a fortnight to allow me to cover my business expenses. Just don't allow it to become a habit!

Get Money Coming In

It goes without saying that generating an income from your new business is essential to keep it afloat. Cash flow is king when it comes to bootstrapping. Make sure the people or business that buy your products or services pay on time. This means making payment options easy and easily repeatable.

Setting up a payment platform that saves credit card details will encourage repeat business with you. There are many options on the market including PayPal, Stripe, eWay and SecurePay, so research these fully as there are always fees involved.

It is important to price your product and services so that they are acceptable for your target market. Investigating any competitors' prices are a good place to start but remember to go back to your financials to ensure that you are covering your costs and can turn a profit. There is no point being the cheapest if you can't sustain it!

Setting your prices correctly at the beginning makes it easier in the long run when you eventually need to increase the price. Let's face it, this will happen as everything keeps costing more!

Financial Opportunities

Get On Email Lists

Grants are offered all the time to encourage small businesses to establish and scale. Business.gov.au is an Australian government site that includes a Grants & Programs finder that suits you. They are favourable to businesses in rural or regional areas, female founders and Aboriginal and Torres Strait Islander peoples.

Grants.gov.au is another place to search for opportunities. There are also grant opportunities offered by large companies that have philanthropic reasons for encouraging start-ups or ideas that can be commercialised.

Talk to Those That Have Been Successful With Grants

Securing funding from grants can be hard! It is essential to read the objectives for the grant and consider if you can meet them before you even start writing your application.

When you start writing, make sure you save your answers as you go, as the website may crash and you can lose hours of work. Better yet, create a secure document of your own that you can build upon and adjust for each grant opportunity as it arises.

Grant applications often seek the same information – what is your business, what problem does it solve, what financials are involved and what is your plan for using the money.

Asking for advice from other businesses that have been awarded grants will give you some insights into what made those applications successful. Ask those people to read over your grants and provide you with feedback to improve your application.

Don't be disheartened if you don't end up on the shortlist. They are often highly competitive and very niche.

If at first you don't succeed …

Invest in a Grant Writer

Go to an expert! There are grant writers who have a wealth of experience in this area. They know how to interpret the eligibility requirements and if you meet them, and how to address the application requirements. You can even work in the costs of grant writing and reporting into your grant application to help you pay for your grant genie (if successful, of course!).

However, you need to give them plenty of notice as it can take weeks or months to prepare a successful grant application. Also, they are likely to be working on more than one application at any one time. Many grant writers can read over your own attempt at grant writing to provide feedback that may save you time and money.

Acquire Capital Investment

You will need to learn to pitch (aka sell) your business to others to get them to invest in you. There are a number of business incubators and accelerators that can help you refine your pitch to ensure that it sells your story and why other people should give you money.

A capital investment is a sum of cash acquired by a company to pursue its objectives. You could try crowdfunding, or the pooling of money from many individuals, in return for equity or rewards.

Angel investors are high-wealth individuals who provide start-up capital, from thousands to hundreds of thousands of dollars, to entrepreneurs in exchange for a percentage of equity in the company. They often also provide mentorship or advice in business, so make sure they know about your industry!

Venture capitalists, like angel investors, exchange start-up capital for equity but often provide later-stage funding, in the millions of dollars, from other people's money, such as pension funds or private equity. It is important that you don't get locked out of your business as it grows by relying too heavily on investors and the distribution of equity.

Mentors and Collaborations

Make Connections Early

The national and local governments love encouraging small business success. They have and continue to fund mentoring opportunities for women in business. It is a priority area for them because we are a largely untapped resource. Often these opportunities are either fully or partially funded.

Consider joining a collaborative workspace in your local town or city so you can bounce ideas of other people and stay motivated. There are also start-up incubators and accelerators that can provide mentors early in your business growth journey.

Look out for other successful business owners and ask them directly if they can offer you advice and support for a set period or in an ongoing capacity. You will be pleasantly surprised how many people are flattered that you consider them as a potential mentor and will happily make space for you in their schedules.

Reach Out for Help

You can't know or do it all, so you will need help at some stage in your business' development and growth. And it doesn't always have to cost money.

Sometimes, other businesses may offer you a trial of their product/service in exchange for feedback, reviews or promotion. This is a great way to support other start-ups by building their marketing through testimonials and allowing them to improve their offering.

Asking about other peoples' experiences or recommendations can save you time and money, as they have often been burnt in their own entrepreneurial journey. Remember, the only silly question is the one that isn't asked.

Offer Your Services

You can consider collaborating or working with another business with similar values and target market. You can look for one that is not a direct competitor and can help to boost both businesses. This collaboration can occur without any exchange of money, saving costs for both.

Consider running a joint competition where you both donate a prize (can be product or service-based) when people sign up to your newsletter. There are plenty of opportunities such as a joint competition, an Instagram live interview or offering a discount code. It gets your business seen by another audience and shows that your business is trustworthy.

Conclusion

PharmOnline is a bootstrapped business, enabling full control over financial decisions and swift adjustments to occur. Initially starting out as a business-to-consumer business, PharmOnline has now morphed into a predominantly business-to-business (B2B) company, to meet the needs of the market.

One of our B2Bs required a fully encapsulated online system for private and secure transfer of medical information, so we invested our money into a product that met these needs and could be used for all of our other services as well.

Although this has been a challenging change to make, money was quickly transferred to be used to create reliable and regular cash flow. This process may have been slower or not possible without this control.

Bootstrapping is a challenging but often a rewarding way of starting your small business. It will take time, passion and perseverance to succeed. You need to plan for all possibilities and be prepared to adapt when you need to. Keep money in reserve for when a crisis occurs!

There are many ways that you can fund your business using this method but make sure you look at all the pros and cons first before relying too much on one type. Wishing you all the best on your own business journey!

About the Author

Anna Barwick, the 2021 NSW Pharmacist of the Year, is a Pharmacy Practice Lecturer in the School of Rural Medicine at the University of New England. Born and raised on an organic and biodynamic property at Peak Hill, Anna now lives with her husband and children on their Australian Stockhorse Stud farm in Walcha. Anna is currently working on her PhD, holds a Master of Clinical Pharmacy, is a practising pharmacist, a researcher and a pharmacist immuniser.

Anna's vision is to put a pharmacist into every household in the country, 24 hours a day, whenever people need help. Anna founded PharmOnline, an online advisory video telehealth service, to connect people with experienced pharmacists to discuss their medication. PharmOnline was awarded the NSW Business New England North West Outstanding Start Up award and was runner up in the NSW AusMumpreneur Digital Innovation award in 2021.

She is passionate about improving the health of all Australians through education, advice and advocacy in her role as a medication expert.

Part 3

Marketing

Chapter Ten
Make Marketing a Priority in Your Business

By Jenn Donovan
Social Media & Marketing Australia

Introduction

If you feel like you're doing all the right things but are just not hitting your targets …

You're in the right place.

You know there's something missing but just can't put your finger on it.

You're in the right place.

You're busy but not productive.

You're in the right place.

Feel like you're posting to crickets.

You're in the right place.

Emailing ad hoc – sometimes Wednesday, sometimes this week or this month, sometimes never!

You're in the right place.

Want a business that you're not chasing your tail, not putting out spot fires, not in overwhelm for most of the day

You're in the right place.

Small business is a tough gig.

No one in small business would ever dispute that.

And as small business owners, we spend a lot of time working *in* our businesses. Doing the daily grind.

The customer service.

The bookkeeping.

The emails.

All the bits.

For some businesses, it's only one person. They are a solopreneur, and the buck literally stops with them because, clearly, there is only them!

Some days the list of things to do is overwhelming and we wonder whether we'll ever get to the bottom of the list.

Hint: You never will – we do something, we tick it off and boom there's more to do. The anguish of the small business owner – the job is never done.

However, if we want our business to grow, we need to make sure that people know about us, our business, what we sell, what we stand for – heck we need to MARKET ourselves.

And with everything I've discussed above, busy being busy and busy working *in* our business, we clearly need to make time to work *on* our business.

It's this "being busy" stuff that prevents a business from growing.

Knee deep in all the doing, and not getting around to the marketing.

Before we go much further into making marketing a priority, however, let's look at what marketing really is. Because just as how branding is more than a logo, marketing is more than just Facebook!

What Is Marketing?

My mentor always taught me that marketing is *everything*.

Because everything you DO and everything you SAY in business says something about you, regardless of whether you mean it to or not.

Read that again. It's one of the most important lines in the chapter!

The way you answer your phone is marketing.

The way you respond to an email is marketing

The way you conduct yourself online is marketing. Yes, even in your personal profile.

Because your audience is always watching. Wondering, "Is this person the person for me?"

People do business with people they *know*, *like* and *trust*.

How do they discover if they know, like and trust you? By watching – watching from the sidelines.

Marketing is everything.

But don't let that scare you.

Embrace it.

If you are a brand that is authentically you. If you are the same person in your business as you would be at the pub on a Friday night (well, within reason), then marketing being everything, isn't scary. Instead, it's something to embrace, learn from and be aware of and will actually be your SUPERPOWER in a competitive and noisy marketplace.

If Marketing Is Everything, How Do I Market My Small Business?

Brilliant question!

The simple answer is that you market your business consistently.

Consistency with branding, including tone, voice, colours and so forth.

Consistency with a message.

Consistency with calls to action (telling them what to do next).

Consistency with strategy, mindset and methodology.

More about all this later in the chapter, I promise!.

Basically, you need to know who your target audience is, where they hang out, what problem you solve for them, what you stand for (brand values). Keeping all of this consistent!

Marketing is simple, but it's not easy!

It takes time, effort, energy and strategy.

But if you crack the code for how to market what you do, to the people who want to buy what you sell, your business HAS to be a success.

Why You Need to Make Marketing a Priority

The answer to why you need to make marketing a priority in your business is simple.

If you want to grow you need to learn to put the *right* message in front of the *right* audience at the *right* time so that they will buy what you sell, and then (this is the kicker) they will not only come back again and again as repeat customers but also be a referrer of business to you and become your biggest fan.

So, basically, if you want to grow, you have to market.

If no one knows about you, about what you sell or why they should buy from you, rather than everyone else who sells what you sell, then you will fail in business.

Marketing is the key to meeting your financial goals – as long as you have a product that people want to buy!

Before we hit the real nitty-gritty of this marketing chapter, let's first look at where you are in your business journey.

Because it is a journey. We are all at different stages of our journey, but we all have a similar endpoint.

Perhaps you're feeling INVISIBLE to your customers in the noisy and busy marketplace we are trying to operate our businesses in.

You have taken the leap – started your dream business and your passion is probably the highest it will ever be (or so you think!). You simply need to be seen more by the right people who you just know need what you sell. You need clients or customers.

> Taking the leap. Starting a new business. Passion is high. Need clients, need to be seen.   INVISIBLE

You are definitely trading time for money. This means that you are spending your time doing the work and the thought of hiring help is a little too far down the track.

Or maybe this is more you.

You're in the ACTIVE phase of your business.

You've got a few good clients.

You've got your fingers crossed that this will work.

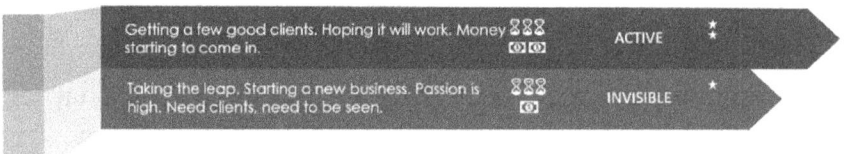

Money has started to come in – so yay for money. Yet you're feeling like you are a hamster on a wheel, doing so much and still trading time for money.

Not you yet?

Well, perhaps you are in the BUSYNESS phase of business.

Busy being busy.

Someone says "Hi, how are you going?" and your standard response is "busy".

You are doing all the right things, doing the daily grind.

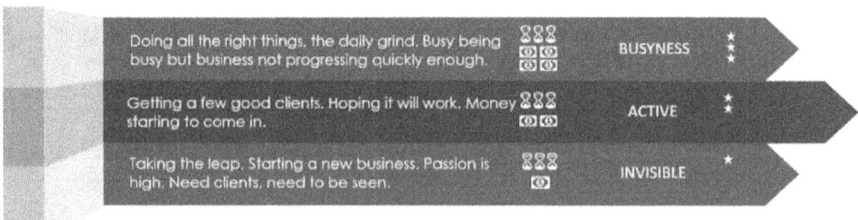

You are busy being busy, but you just feel like you aren't progressing quickly enough. This business thing is starting to get frustrating.

You feel that you should be further along.

After all, you are doing everything the experts tell you, but still, you are trading time for money and still feeling like not enough people can see you – despite all the posting on social media, all the email campaigns, all the marketing.

The next phase of business is CLARITY.

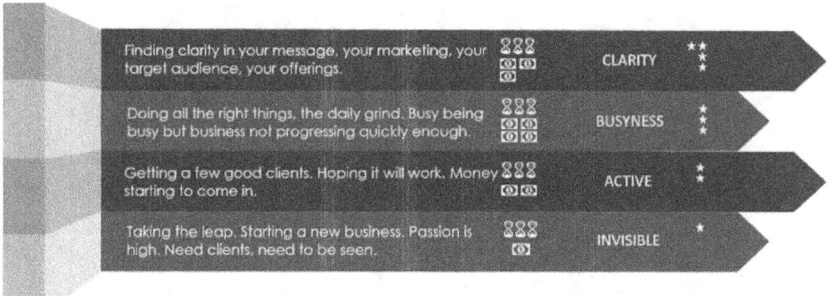

In this phase you are starting to see clarity in your message to the market, you have clarity over what you are selling and the people you need to attract to buy what you sell.

You understand your target market more and more, you have clarity over your offerings and what makes you different in the marketplace. People know what you sell and how to buy from you.

You are making yourself easy to buy from.

You are no longer trading time for money – you now have the cash flow to hire some help – even just a few hours a week.

In the clarity phase, everything feels like it's coming together.

Or maybe this is you.

You are in the INFLUENTIAL phase of your business.

You're in control, on-brand, attracting ALL the right clients and are becoming the GO-TO person in your industry.

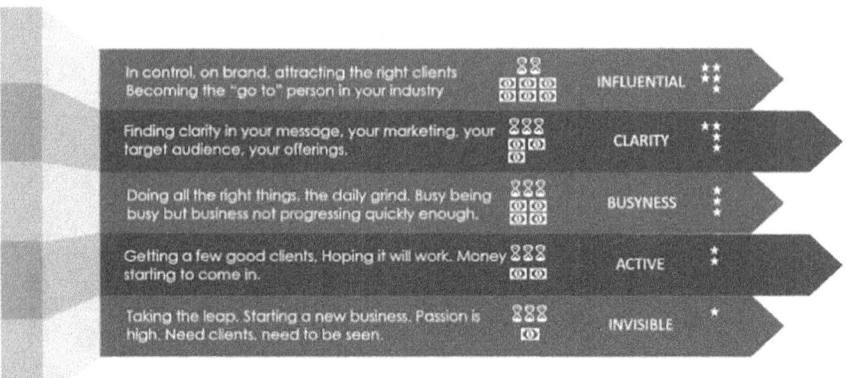

You have hired help to do many of the tasks that aren't "money-making activities", and you are no longer trading time for money.

You recognise your worth and people are prepared to pay for your expertise.

The last level, and if you're here, crack open a bottle of champers because you are amazing!

You are INVINCIBLE.

You are in love with your business, and you are working less and earning more.

Your business is giving you exactly what you wanted when you first started out.

The income you deserve and the freedom.

The Journey of the Business Owner
Where are you on this scale at the moment?

In love with your business, working less, earning more, enjoying the lifestyle.	INVINCIBLE
In control, on brand, attracting the right clients. Becoming the "go to" person in your industry.	INFLUENTIAL
Finding clarity in your message, your marketing, your target audience, your offerings.	CLARITY
Doing all the right things, the daily grind. Busy being busy but business not progressing quickly enough.	BUSYNESS
Getting a few good clients. Hoping it will work. Money starting to come in.	ACTIVE
Taking the leap. Starting a new business. Passion is high. Need clients, need to be seen.	INVISIBLE

You are enjoying the lifestyle you created.

Your internal or external team is now an integral part of your business and the only work you really do is the work that makes you money.

You have now gone from being INVISIBLE to being INVINCIBLE in the marketplace.

This is where all small business owners want to get to.

If we didn't want freedom and the ability to be paid what we are worth, then we would have stayed in a JOB.

Where do you sit in the business owner journey?

Four Out of Five Small Businesses Fail in the First Five Years

The statistic we hear all the time is that four out of five small businesses fail in the first five years.

That's 80% of people who have a great idea for a business or push themselves outside their comfort zone and start a business that *fails*.

Of that 80%, sadly 95% of them are women in business.

Yet the reality, in my view, is quite different.

They DON'T fail.

They simply BURN OUT.

In the first five years, 80% of small business owners can't get enough customers to buy enough products and to come back often enough to make being in business profitable and worth the energy.

So, they quit and get a job.

Getting enough leads to convert enough customers and getting enough customers to convert into repeat customers is too hard and leads to burnout in the process.

So, what's the solution?

You know what I'm going to say – it's what the chapter is all about.

The solution is MARKETING.

If these small business owners made marketing a priority in their business, not a sometimes activity or a "when I get time" activity, if these small business owners worked more *on* their business than *in* their business, more would survive and less would burn out.

I know, it sounds so simple.

And it is.

Doesn't make it easy though – just simple.

In Part 4 of this chapter, we talk about the four Ingredients to Marketing Success, and I can't wait to share it all with you. For a bit of context, against the idea of failing and making marketing a priority, let's look at the science.

In business, we need to know the answers to the following three really important questions:

1. Who is my "who"?
2. What do I want to be famous for?
3. Where does my "who" hang out?

The answer to these questions gives you your message, your market and pieces of your strategy.

More on this later.

Aside from strategy, we need to know our numbers in business.

We need to know how many leads we need to get into our business in order to convert enough leads into paying customers, to make a profit.

If we know our conversion rate (rate of converting leads into paying customers) is 10%, then we know that for every hundred leads, we will get ten paying customers.

Leads could be new people to our email list, new members to our private Facebook group, new qualified follows on Instagram or people through the doors of our bricks-and-mortar business.

And if we also know that our average customer spend is $65 (average customer spend is worked out by dividing our gross income profit by the number of clients we have), then for every hundred clients/customers we will bring in $6,500.

Stick with me here.

If we want to double our income, in the simplest form, we need to double our qualified leads.

So, how do you get two hundred new leads as opposed to one hundred?

Or how do you increase your average customer spend from $65 to $85?

Drum roll …

You know it's coming.

Marketing.

How to Make Marketing a Priority

I hope in the first 2,000 odd words here, I've managed to convince you of the power of marketing, the power of making marketing a priority and the power of working *on* your business, as opposed to always working *in* your business.

I'm sure one of the biggest questions you currently have circling your mind is "how?" How do I make marketing a priority?

With the limited time I have around running the business, running a family, running a household, working full-time/part-time, etc, how am I supposed to do this Jenn?

Here are some thoughts.

Carve Out Time for Marketing

I love marketing. I live it, breathe it, dream about it. Yet I still have to carve out time for it.

It's not something that happens naturally for me, but I carve out time because I know its power.

I know if I want to grow my business, I have to market.

So, sometimes for me, it's Sunday afternoon and other times it's Monday – in fact almost all-day Monday that I dedicate to marketing.

I look at what my theme is for the week or month, head to Canva and make some social media tiles, write some copy and schedule for my posts for the week – or if I'm really enthusiastic for a fortnight or so.

Theming helps me create content.

As I record a podcast weekly (Small Business Made Simple), most of my social content is based around that theme for the week.

Whatever my podcast is about, I post about it.

But I also have other themes that come from my goals.

I talk more about themes in the strategy section below – in Taking Marketing Action.

As a super quick overview of my goals versus my strategy, here's what that looks like.

Goal: To speak more on stage.

Strategy example: One post per fortnight talking about past speaking gigs, saying why someone should pick me for their speaking event, sending people to my Speakers Page.

Call to action: Book Jenn to speak!

Goal: To become the go-to person in my industry.

Strategy example: #tipstuesday, storytelling, lessons I've learnt posts, reach out strategy (commenting and helping others).

You start to get the picture.

And although we don't really talk about setting goals in this chapter, they certainly form an important part of your marketing strategy.

To carve out time is as simple as booking an appointment with yourself to do marketing.

Ok, it's not that simple but it should be. If you had a client appointment or a doctor's appointment booked, you'd stick to it – so make yourself a priority and book a consistent appointment with yourself, either daily, weekly or monthly – depending on how you like to work.

Daily might not work – but you do you. If doing five minutes a day is more achievable than giving up half a day each fortnight, then do that.

I guess the whole point is, if you aren't carving out any time right now for marketing, any amount of time from here on in is better than what you are currently doing.

Outsourcing

Of course, the next option is to outsource your marketing to someone else.

Someone whose expertise is in marketing and can help you level up your business.

If you can make room in your budget, outsourcing can be a fabulous option to help you make marketing a priority in your business.

However, I'm aware that it's not as perfect as it sounds.

You can't, or rarely can you, simply outsource your marketing and have it all done for you.

Unless this person is someone who knows your business back to front, your goals, your ideal client and what you want to be famous for and so forth, you are still going to have to provide content.

Although outsourcing seems like the perfect solution, it won't help if you don't have a strategy (fancy word for a plan) for your marketing!

If you do have a plan, or the person you are outsourcing to can help you with a plan to help you reach your goals, this could be the best investment you make in your business.

My advice with outsourcing is to test and measure. Don't go all in and sign a 12-month contract with someone – make sure they are a good fit for you and that they align with your branding and, in particular, your brand's tone and your business values.

Oh, and it's wise to remember that you get what you pay for! If you want someone to do three posts on social media a week for $50 – you'll get what you paid for.

With posts taking around thirty minutes or more each to create, build assets for, write engaging copy, research, upload and schedule – you are only paying around $17 per hour – and you will get the quality of $17 per hour.

Just think about it.

Tools to Make Life Simpler

If you decide that outsourcing is either out of the budget or just not for you, and that you want to market yourself, then here are some tools (at the time of writing this chapter) I would recommend you invest in.

And I do mean invest.

Free is great when you need free.

Tools that have a free level are great when you are starting out and this is what you can afford, but you are trading time for money.

When you have the cash flow to upgrade to a paid version of something, you will begin to trade money for time. That is, you paid more to get more time back, because paid versions have more tools and resources to help you save time.

When you can afford it – and realise that paying $150 per year for a tool that can save you five hours a week and your hourly charge rate is $95 an hour – you can soon see that the tool is a fabulous investment!

1.   A Graphic Design Tool

We can't all afford to hire a graphic designer. A program that helps you design great graphics, easily helps you keep on brand (colours, fonts, etc) and has amazing templates is an essential tool to have in your toolbox.

Programs I'd suggest are:

- Photoshop (in the Adobe Suite)
- Canva (www.canva.com)
- Adobe Spark
- WordSwag (an app in your app store)

I know that there's hundreds more and you might ask your community which one they use and love and go on their recommendation.

My recommendation is Canva. It's an Australian design company (I'm always up for supporting Australian entrepreneurs wherever I can!) and well, it's simply brilliant.

As someone who's graphically challenged, Canva makes me look fabulous!

It has a great free version, but the paid version will simplify your life even more. Totally worth the investment.

2. A Social Media Scheduler

Whenever I talk about using social media schedulers, the first question I get asked is, "Will scheduling get less favour in the algorithm than posting directly onto the platform?".

My answer is simply, I don't know!

My long-winded answer is to forget the algorithm to a certain extent and think to yourself, if I don't schedule and therefore don't post, how much algorithm am I missing out on then?

It's better to post via scheduling, than not post at all!

Like graphic design tools, there's plenty – and I mean plenty – of social media schedulers out there.

Here's a few I've used in the past or still use now:

- Planoly
- Later
- Facebook Creator Studio
- Buffer
- Sociamonials
- Hootesuite
- Canva (yep, on the paid version it has its own scheduler)
- Facebook's inbuilt scheduling tool for Facebook and Instagram
- Meet Edgar

I'm no expert on scheduling tools. I've used a lot over the years and honestly, I haven't found the perfect one, which is why I use a few different tools.

They range in price but most have a freemium level (free level).

What you choose depends on what platforms you want to schedule on, and even on those platforms, what type of content you are wanting to schedule – stories, posts into the feed, videos, reels and so on.

As with most marketing, finding the perfect scheduling tool requires testing and measuring and listening to the stories of others that have gone before you!

Just like a graphic design tool, looking for free options is a great way to start, but once you can budget to spend money on one of their paid packages, you will begin to see the amount of time you are saving through just a small monthly or annual investment.

PS, if you do use a scheduling tool, make sure you make time to go and engage on the social platforms too. Posting is one thing, having an outreach strategy where you interact and build trust with others is a whole other strategy and time-consuming piece of marketing that you need to do!

1. Email Campaign Program

It might surprise you to learn that not all marketing is done on social media!

Queue the astonishment sound effect!

Email marketing should form a very important part of your strategic marketing plan. Having an email marketing program is the best way to ensure your emails are sent, seen, opened, read and clicked on.

Just like all the tools I mentioned above, there's a billion email marketing programs out there – ranging in price and therefore ranging in capabilities.

But like everything, we don't know what we don't know, so starting off small is good.

Work out what you want your email program to do for you and hunt for a program that can help.

Here's a few I've used and worked with over the years:

- Mailchimp
- Flodesk
- Campaign Monitor
- Active Campaign
- Convert Kit
- Constant Contact
- Mailerlite
- Keap (formally known as Infusionsoft)

Prices range from free to over $400 a month depending on the size of your email list and the functions and diversity you need in your email marketing.

Again, free might be a good start when you are starting out, but as you grow your business, investing in a paid version is a great business decision.

The analytics you get from paid versions of programs, that can help you make strategic decisions, means your payment pays for itself tenfold over time!

Marketing needs to be a priority in your business.

You're only halfway through this chapter, and you've heard that a least six times I'm sure.

And although you might think that I'm repeating myself, and I am, but the consequences of not getting the message and not taking action are unfathomable to me.

Somewhere near the start of this chapter on marketing, I wrote that about 80% of small businesses fail and 95% of them being women owned. That, to put it bluntly, is the result that NOT making marketing a priority can bring.

After reading this chapter, if all you do is take more action towards your marketing, even if it's not perfect (and let's face it, perfect doesn't exist), then my job will be done.

I want success for you and your business.

Buyers need what you sell, you just need to seek them out and show them why you're the exact person they need in their life to solve their problem.

Marketing – it's everything.

Key Ingredients to Marketing Success

The number one thing to help you make your business a success is marketing.

And there are four key ingredients within marketing to attribute to that success.

These are:
- Your message
- Your strategy
- Your methods
- Your mindset

So, let's dig a little deeper into how they help with marketing success.

Your Message

This is all about getting your message across to your target market so that buyers will buy!

Simple, right?

Well, yes, but, as usual, not easy to begin with.

When looking at your message to your target market, we need to answer clearly and in some depth these questions:

1. Who is your who? In other words, who is your ideal client and customer avatar? Who is it that you think is most likely to need or want what you sell?

2. What do you want to be famous for? I'm not talking about Beyoncé famous, but if there was a room of your ideal clients talking about you and your business, what would they say? Do they know what you do, what you sell and what problem you solve? Is your branding clear? Are you easy to buy from?

3. What kind of BRAND are you? What are your core business values? What do you stand for? Is your brand serious, fun, bright, shiny or professional?

4. What are the problems and challenges you solve for your customer or clients?

5. Is your business scalable? You can have the best idea, the best business plan and the best marketing strategy, but if your business isn't scalable, then you are destined to fail.

To help you out, as we go through, you can visit https://bit.ly/JennsWorkbook to download the workbook to help you work through your message, branding, strategy, method and mindset.

Your Strategy

Marketing without strategy is like travelling the world without a map or Google. You know where you want to get to, and you'll probably eventually get there, but if you just had a map you'd save time, energy and money getting there!

A good marketing strategy comes from working out your goals – financial goals and more – and working backwards from there until you have a roadmap of how to achieve that goal.

Firstly, set your goals – your big hairy audacious goals (BHAGs).

Set your annual goals that will help you achieve your BHAGs.

From your annual goals, break them down into quarterly goals with action steps under each one.

Then break your quarterly goals into monthly goals, again with steps under them, and then monthly into weekly and possibly daily goals and steps, if that helps you and works well for you!

Let's use an example in my business.

If my goal is to have my podcast downloaded 200,000 times, then simply doing a weekly podcast won't be enough.

I need a strategy on how I will market the podcast to reach enough audience members to hit my download goal.

If I want 200,000 downloads in one year, that means 50,000 downloads a quarter, 17,000 a month, or 600 a day.

So, what marketing strategy can I undertake to reach at least 600 listeners a day.

How many posts on social media is that? How many emails is that? What's the paid strategy versus the organic strategy?

What's the reach out strategy? What guests can I have on that would promote my podcast to their audience?

The goal of 200,000 listeners in twelve months seems so big, but when you break them down into daily goals, it seems much more achievable.

To form a good strategy, we look back on our messaging as well.

What do we want to be famous for?

What are we an expert in?

What problems or challenges do we solve for our customers or client?

Breaking your goals down from BHAGs into doable, daily or weekly step by step actions ensures everything you do in your marketing is moving you and your business closer to success and achieving the goals you set out to achieve when you started.

Now doesn't that sound better than closing your computer at 5 pm on Friday afternoon thinking, "Darn it, I didn't post on social media *again* this week! I'll try again next week …"

Your Methods

This is probably my favourite key ingredient to successful marketing. It just makes so much sense, and this is where most of the aha moments come from when speaking to clients and audiences.

Your marketing method involves knowing:

- What platforms you should be on.
- What other marketing approaches do you need to take, for example, email marketing or podcasting sponsorship

- Where your ideal client hangs out, in order for you to market to them.
- When to look outside the square with your marketing to stand out from the crowded and noisy marketplace.

When I say I love this key ingredient the most because of the aha moments, it's because when you work out the answers to these questions, marketing becomes simple.

Many small business owners I come across have never really thought about why they are on, for instance, Instagram or what part of Instagram they are using – Stories, feed, IGTV and so on.

They are simply following the trends or listening to so-called experts giving general advice.

When questioned about why they are posting on Instagram the answers are, "Because everyone is" or "I didn't want to miss out".

The answer of course should be, for example, "Because my ideal buyer is on there and they love watching and interacting with stories and direct messages".

I am also a fan of working out your marketing method because we get stuck thinking that social media is our only marketing strategy but in reality, building empires on crown land (land that you don't own) is a seriously bad idea!

So, when small business owners start to look at sponsoring podcasts that their ideal audience listens to, invest money into a Google Ad campaign or start to use Google My Business to their strategic advantage, it not only lights them up but it lights me up too!

Thinking about your marketing method is knowing your ideal client or customer so well that you know where to market to them and can do so at the right time with the right message to get the sale or the desired action taken.

Your Mindset

To a certain degree, this whole chapter is about your marketing mindset.

If you can change your mindset from marketing being a "sometimes activity" or a "when I get time activity" to an "I will make marketing a priority in my business", then you have the mindset ingredient of marketing 90% covered!

But if you aren't making marketing a priority, then perhaps you need to ask and deal with questions such as:

1. What are the roadblocks to your success?

2. What are your roadblocks to attracting your ideal client/customer?

3. What is the result of not dealing with these roadblocks?

4. What does success look like to you?

5. Actual outcomes versus desired outcomes – where is the disconnect?

Everyone has a different idea of what success for them looks like.

That's why it's so important to define success for yourself. Not what others think or see or do, but what success is to you.

What would success feel like?

What would success look like?

What would success look like in monetary value?

The reality of success is that we are most likely the roadblock to our own success.

We are standing in our own way.

Perhaps that's because we don't have the skills yet, don't have the cash flow to hire the people we need to, or don't have the belief in ourselves to give this business thing a "red hot go"!

We need to work on ourselves, surround ourselves with the best people available who will push us, challenge us and celebrate with us.

A roadblock is just that. Imagine a blockage in the road you take every day to work, the office or to the supermarket. Think how frustrating that would be if you had to go 30 minutes out of your way every day because of the roadblock.

If someone would just get rid of it or move it, life would be easier, happier and you'd feel less stressed.

Whether you invest in a mentor, business coach, life coach, an online program or just start listening to a helpful podcast or two to help you remove your own roadblocks, the simple action of starting and taking action might be all you need to move closer to your own version of success.

We invest in programs around marketing, social media, finances and so on, investing in your mindset, as a business owner, can be one of the best improvements you do for both you and your business.

Mindset plays an enormous part in marketing success.

Time to Take Action

When it comes to marketing and taking action, there are three things I think you need to do – I call them the Three S's of Action:

1. Show Up: You need to show up for your audience.

2. Strategy: You need a marketing strategy.

3. Sell: You need a selling/business mindset.

Show Up

In marketing, I talk a lot about H2H Marketing – Human to Human Marketing.

People do business with people they know, like and trust.

Put simply, if you're not showing up for your audience, then how can they get to know you, like you and trust you.

We need to make sure we are showing up for our audience.

Does this mean video?

Yes.

Does it mean ALL video?

No.

But video is king and has been for as long as I've been teaching digital marketing, and I can't see that changing any time soon.

If you're thinking, *no way Jenn, I'm not getting on video*, then let me tell you a little story!

Some years ago, I was involved in a mastermind program, and this particular day at lunchtime, our challenge was to do a live Facebook video (I was horrified!).

My friend Sam and I went for lunch, I procrastinated for about forty-five minutes, whining about having to do it and how I didn't like my voice or my face on video and *blah blah blah* – every excuse under the sun.

Sam turned to me and said "Jenn, what you have to realise is that you sound and look the same sitting here talking to me right now, as you do on video. So, if you don't feel uncomfortable talking to me now, why is the video any different?"

Sam made me cry that day.

I cried because he was right, and I cried because I was grieving any chance of an excuse from that day forward.

He was right (but don't tell him that!).

Although I still don't like video, I do video.

I do video because I know its power as a marketing tactic.

There's just no disputing it.

It's eye-catching, it's human, it's engaging, it's expertise building, it's the king of content.

So, here's your chapter challenge!

Go live or pre-record a video of you telling your audience three things they don't know about you and put it out there!

Be sure to tag me – I'll cheer you on for sure!

If you hate it, put it out there and never watch it again!

But like I said, it doesn't have to be all video.

I would advise investing a few hundred dollars as soon as possible in your business journey to get some branded professional photos done of yourself, and you in your work environment, or other appropriate photos that show your personality and what you do.

Start showing up for your audience.

I promise you that it will be some of the most engaging marketing content you do.

If you've never shown up for your audience, then you are going to be blown away by the response!

Just think, if you had a bricks-and-mortar store, you'd have to show up every day. Don't use your online presence as an excuse to not show up for the people who know, like and trust you and want to buy from you!

Strategy

I've talked a lot about strategy throughout the chapter.

You need a strategy, and the essence of that strategy is to help you reach your business goals – whatever they are.

Strategy, like marketing, will take time. But this is part of the time you need to be working *on* your business, not *in* your business.

The strategy will make your business life simpler, sales easier and goal ticking a breeze!

If you don't know where to start, reach out. Reach out for a strategy session, if not with me, then with someone you trust to help you.

Your future self will thank you for it!

Sell

We hear people talk about sales and marketing, but in reality, it's marketing and sales.

Marketing brings in the leads, so the sale can be done.

And although marketing isn't about selling, it is about building quality leads so that when we ask for the sale, there are fewer objections, and the sale is easier to close.

So many small business owners spend all their time in nurture mode – never asking for the sale.

Others are always selling – buy this, buy that, buy from me!

No one likes to be sold to all the time!

But if we never ask for the sale, we aren't making ourselves easy to buy from.

And making yourself easy to buy from is one key to getting the sale in the first place.

Even at times when you don't have anything to sell – you can still ask for the sale through your calls to action.

Calls to action could be "buy this", of course, but they could also be micro-conversions, which lead to a sale, like:

- "Try for free"
- "Comment below"
- "Download my Freebie guide"
- "Sign up for my newsletter"
- "Learn more"
- "Give us a call"
- "Follow/Like/Connect"
- "Keep me informed"
- "Listen to the podcast"

Oh, the list of calls to action is endless!

And although these are not asking directly for the exchange of money, they are asking your audience to come deeper into your world, get to know you a little more, get to know your expertise a little more and trust you a little more.

So, the sale isn't always about the dollars, the sale is sometimes about the micro-conversion action taken to deepen a relationship with a future prospect.

When you post on social media or send out an email, what's the call to action? What are you asking the person, who has stopped and read your marketing message, to do next?

Don't leave them hanging – make sure you are asking for another action step.

Before I leave you to implement the steps you need to make sure your marketing is not only a priority but targeted at the right audience at the right time, with the right message, and with an irresistible call to action, I want to leave you with some advice my mentor taught me.

Ready, fire, aim.

The world doesn't need more people "planning" or "aiming" to do something.

The world needs more action takers.

And that's what I want for you.

After reading this chapter, or after reading all the chapters in this book about building a business, I want you to take some action.

Don't wait for perfection – that's a trap.

It doesn't exist. What's perfect for me, won't be perfect for you, so why try to be perfect?

As a final exercise, to show you the power of marketing, I want you to draw a line on a piece of paper.

On one end of the line, I want you to write the word "novice" and on the other end the word "expert".

Then put a dot midway along the line. Taking the line as a scale of one to ten.

Then I want you to ask yourself these two questions and put a mark along the line for your answer:

- How good are you at what you do?
- How good are you at marketing what you do?

My guess is that you put yourself at around a seven or eight for how good you are at what you do and around a three or four for how good you are at marketing what you do.

How'd I go?

The gap between how good you are at what you do and how good you are at marketing what you do, is the gap that kills four out of five businesses in the first five years.

It's not that you aren't freaking awesome at what you do, or that you're not an expert at what you do, it's that not enough people know how awesome your business is or why they need your product or service.

Fill the gap.

Make marketing a priority.

About the Author

Jenn Donovan, marketing thought leader, change maker, coach and mentor for small businesses, International Keynote Speaker, Podcaster (Small Business Made Simple – over 150 episodes and growing!) and now officially an author! YAY!

Founder of Social Media and Marketing Australia, founder of the extremely successful community Facebook group – Buy From a Bush Business (over 350,000 members) and the Co-Founder of Social Enterprise Spend With Us – Australia's answer to Amazon but only for rural and regional small businesses.

Jenn's takes her clients from Invisible to Invincible and is also a community leader, and a community believer and is on a mission to ensure the lost art of Human to Human marketing and community are seeded firmly in everyone's marketing strategy in 2021 and beyond.

Jenn has spent over 12 years building businesses, from being a Property Law Specialist to a Retailer to now a mentor and momentum creator! She has built businesses through all the peaks and troughs, the booms and the busts and is now doing the doing, on the ground, helping other small businesses.

Her love for marketing and social media is clear to anyone in her world and she knows that if you can get your marketing right (online and offline), and make it a priority, you can build the business of your dreams, get paid what you deserve and make a bigger difference to the world.

Jenn's philosophy and values around this, making marketing a priority, is exactly why she wrote the chapter on marketing that she did. It's such an important message for any business owner – no matter how long they have been in business.

Jenn lives on a farm in the Riverina of NSW, Australia, with husband Ruston and their three children. Jenn has ten chooks, two peacocks, two guinea fowl, one dog and one cat and several pet lambs – she's banned from going around the sheep in lambing season now!

Connect with Jenn on Instagram @jenndonovan and LinkedIn @jenndonovan_ or join her Facebook group Like Minded Business Owners – a community of people like you!

Chapter Eleven
Copywriting Essentials for Rural Businesses

By Sarah Walkerden
The Rural Copywriter / The Rural Marketing Company

Why Is Copywriting Important?

Copywriting is communication. And communicating the right messages to the right people is paramount. Or at least, it is if you want your marketing, and indeed your business, to truly succeed.

What you say is important. But *how* you say it can be even more important. Just like how there might be fifty ways to skin a cat (not literally!), there is more than one way of saying the same thing. However, the way you say things will either connect with certain audiences more or less.

So, the trick is to know precisely *how* to talk to *your* ideal audience. This is how you'll get the sales, bookings or enquiries.

Now, the more specific you can make your target audience, the better. Or at least, generally speaking, this is the case. Be careful that you do not go too narrow.

Once you can specify who you want to target, it becomes much easier to specifically craft marketing messages for them. This makes your message much more effective.

Many business owners neglect this part of the business puzzle. Particularly, when it comes to website copywriting. They go through great pains to design a good-looking website, built by a professional, throw up a few descriptions of their products or services and who they are, and that's about it.

Something along the lines of "Welcome to 'such and such' website. I am Kelly. And my products are blue." That type of copy is really quite boring. It does nothing to attract or engage a customer.

Poorly written copy can ruin a good-looking website. Our website is the first place that people look to learn about our business. Our website represents our businesses image, and we need one that works. We need a website that converts and sells!

Yes, copywriting is important. And if you combine a great business idea and model with a professional, good-looking website with professional interest-grabbing and connecting copy, your business will thrive. It will put you firmly ahead of your competitors who don't bother with this important step, and it will help you to stand out from them, for who you truly are.

Likewise, if you are writing social media posts, printed advertising or pretty much anything, your copy is the most important factor as to whether anyone takes any notice.

So, let's get started on *how* you write effective copy.

Basic Sales Psychology Principles to Guide Your Writing

Like it or not, copywriting is all about sales. Yes, you also want to attract interest from the right people, get them to read and engage with your content, but you will ultimately want them to do something for you.

And it is the "do something" part that you need to focus on first. You always need a call to action.

That call to action might not necessarily always be to buy something – but even when you are asking people to download a free report, or book in for a strategy call, even when something is free, you still have to sell it. It is still a "conversion", which is still a "sale".

If you feel like you hate sales, you better get over that one quick smart if you want to be successful in business (#*toughlove*). But before you start to worry, we are not about to make you incorporate sleezy tactics, become grimy used-car salespeople or anything along those lines.

Sales = serving. It is that simple. You cannot help your audience, clients or customers unless you serve them in some way. Helping equals serving. And serving equals sales.

And making sales through your copywriting is all about establishing that all important emotional connection.

Remember this copywriting motto: emotion sells, facts back up.

In other words, people buy based off an emotional response *first*, and then use factual information to justify their emotional decision.

Therefore, you lead with the emotional component of what you sell, and the technical specifications and all the factual information comes after. This is where a lot of ecommerce stores get their product descriptions wrong. They throw up a list of features and wonder why they don't sell!

Secondly, to get the emotional response that you will need to sell a product or service, you need to dig deep into the outcomes or end-product that the purchaser will receive or achieve.

You are not trying to sell a coaching process, for example – you are selling a tangible and specific outcome that they will receive at the end of that coaching process.

This might be:

- To find love.
- To make more money.
- To train a horse better so that he performs better without bucking them off(!).

… that type of thing.

But here is where you need to be careful and quite specific.

Take weight loss for instance. If someone wants to lose weight, it's not really about the weight. It is – but it isn't. It's really about fitting into nicer clothes. It's about feeling better about the way they look. It's about feeling healthier. It's about having the energy to run around and play with their kids without collapsing in a heap on the ground.

Instead of focusing on "I can help you lose weight", you would be better off focusing on "I can help you shed ten kilos so you can feel great, gain more energy and keep up with your kids, no matter how active they might be."

Hopefully, you can see the difference.

Writing for the Rural Audience

Copywriting for a rural audience can be vastly different to writing for a city-based audience. This is because our lifestyles are vastly different and therefore, we have different priorities and motivations.

For example, talking to a farmer who works sixteen-hour days out in all types of weather conditions, six to seven days a week, is very different from talking to a city corporate who works from nine to five, sitting at a desk and wearing a suit, with their weekends spent relaxing and drinking coffee.

However, a rural audience is not just about farmers. There are many different types of rural audiences and "country folk" that you may need to be aware of. Here are a few you might like to think about …

Regional Audiences

'Regional' can be very different to "rural". Regional audiences might live in a larger country city or town, such as Ballarat, Bendigo or Albury, so they are still close to plenty of modern conveniences such as clothing shops, hardware stores and decent supermarkets. They are merely not in a major capital city. Otherwise, they are likely to live in a more suburban house without land or on a few acres just outside of it.

Tree Changers and Retirees

These are people that have chosen to live outside the city for a country escape. Generally, these folks will be on one to ten acres of land and still in close proximity to a major city centre.

They might have a few hobby animals to keep the grass down and enjoy pottering about the garden or on the ride-on mower.

Rural (But Not Farmers) Audiences

These guys and girls might have around twenty to seventy-five acres of land, with a few horses and other animals. They value being outside of major cities and towns.

They are not necessarily farmers, but they are definitely enthusiastic about living rurally and often have plans to get into farming in future.

Hobby or Small-Scale Farmers

Those who perhaps have 100 to 200 acres, with a basic menagerie of sheep, cows, alpacas, horses or the like. They might breed, milk and make a variety of produce from their animals and/or land.

Commercial Farmers

They are the big guns of agriculture, who run thousands of acres of crops, livestock or both. Commercial farmers have very different lifestyles and priorities.

Remote Residents

They live several hours from civilisation or their closest town. It may be an eight-hour drive to the closest shops, or four hours by helicopter. They have vastly different priorities from someone who lives just thirty minutes from town.

Horse Enthusiasts

Many rural and regional people own, breed and ride horses – either for fun or as a professional sport.

If you're targeting "horse people", it is a good idea to make sure you are targeting the right type. You might choose:

- English riders: dressage riders, show jumping riders, eventing riders, pleasure English riders, pony clubbers, adult riding clubbers
- Western riders: cutting riders, reining riders, bronc riders, Western show riders, Western pleasure riders, Western trail riders, extreme cowboy racing riders
- Stock riders: drovers, musterers, station hand
- Cart drivers
- Thoroughbred racers

- Standardbred or harness racers
- Horse lovers who own horses but do not ride at all
- Horse breeders
- Or a combination of the above

Farmers

The different types of farming are really important aspects to understand if you are targeting farming and agriculture. Different farmers will clearly have different types of lifestyles and challenges, different types of equipment, different types of water and irrigation, different types of soil and terrain.

Generally, farmers do not take too kindly if you do not speak the right language to them! They do not have time for "bulldust", and they make pretty quick assumptions as to how well you understand what they do.

Some of the groups might include:

- Horticulture farmers (vegetables, fruit, olives)
- Viticulture farmers (grapes, wine)
- Crop farmers (grains such as wheat, barley, oats, rice; and hay such as horse hay, cow hay, oaten hay)
- Livestock farmers (wool sheep, meat sheep, dairy cows, meat cows, horses, egg chickens, meat chickens, alpacas, goats)

Yet, it is wise to keep in mind that many farming enterprises are mixed – they grow a few different things and raise various types of livestock.

Here are a few other tips to keep in mind about country folks – keeping in mind that these are generalisations.

In the country, we tend to be:

Humble: They don't like to brag.

Community-minded: They look after their neighbours.

No time for bulldust: One of my favourite sayings, they do not like to beat around the bush or put up with fluffy, unclear language, or pushy sales tactics. Give it to them straight, right now!

Genuine connections: They value genuine connections. They are quite intuitive and can assess whether someone is truly genuine or not in about three seconds. Be yourself, ditch any pretence and be honest, or country folk will soon dismiss you as a fake.

Common challenges: Unrealiable mobile phone reception, internet access and speed; physical isolation; longer travel times for daily activities; and a lack of easy access to common products.

All of this makes a difference to what you should say and how you should say it. Make sure you are talking to people in the right ways, or you will not get results.

Finding Your Writing Style and Your Brand's Tone of Voice

Everyone tends to have their own unique writing style that reflects their unique personality. And this can change and develop over time, the more you write and become comfortable with your own writing. Over time, you will also become more comfortable and confident in articulating what you do and offer in your business.

Hence, the trick to honing your copywriting abilities is to write as much as you possibly can, as often as you can, even if it is your daily social media posts or your weekly blog article.

Know that your first attempts might feel a bit rough or clumsy. This is normal. Like any skill, it takes time and practise. If you persist, it is inevitable that you will find your "flow" and your very own "style".

And as you gradually take more risks and allow your uniqueness to flow into your writing, you will also find that you can magically connect with your customers more.

That's one side to the story.

The other is that many copywriters offer a service called "tone of voice". The copywriter will put together a comprehensive document, with guidelines for your messaging and brand writing style.

If you are really stuck, this can be quite helpful. A tone of voice document can give you a little more structure and confidence around how you want to present your brand through your messaging and give you a lot of tips and tricks to keep it consistent.

While I only do this for my clients from time to time as needed, other copywriters swear by it and promote it as a necessary part of the copywriting process.

My thoughts are this.

If you are nervous about writing for your business and feel more comfortable with having some structure and guidelines, you can engage a copywriter to produce a tone of voice document.

A tone of voice guide will also help if you are planning on outsourcing a significant chunk of your copywriting to one or multiple writers. This will help guide and keep them all consistent to your brand.

The tone of voice document is also useful as you grow into a bigger business with a larger team as it keeps everyone on the same page and your messaging as consistent as possible.

However, if you are the type of small business owner who likes to maintain a close and personal relationship with your customers and clients (a very good strategy to have), you may not need it, or at least not initially.

I tend to believe in authenticity, realness and rawness – as that is what breeds a true connection with your audience. Formal guidelines may restrict this natural creativity and connection.

And often, you simply need to write, write and write some more until you find your writing style and figure out what works for your customers and what feels good to you.

This also depends on the type of person you are.

I am a creative, in-the-moment type of person with quite a quirky writing style (if you haven't noticed!) and I personally, do not need a tone of voice document for my businesses.

I have also found that because I came from a very formal corporate writing background (think government), it took time and practise to really let my personality shine through.

It is a confidence thing really, where you gradually throw off those formal shackles and give yourself permission to just express yourself, your way.

Yet, many business owners find that they need some structure and guidelines to help them, particularly if writing is not their natural strong point (I'd probably put my darling husband in this category as being someone who prefers structure to work with as it gives him more certainty. These days though, I have trained and encouraged him enough that he gives his writing a good go for his metals business – and gets me to edit it).

The main thing is that you find a way of developing your communication and writing style in a way that works for you and your business.

There is a chance that your business *must* be more formal and that is fine too. But for many businesses, you will connect more with your audience when you are a little bit quirky and brave enough to have a little fun.

The Writing Process

This is one of my favourite topics, as I so often hear my clients say, "I'm just not a good writer. I never know what to write. I feel so stuck staring at a blank screen." Here are a few copywriting tricks to beat that blank page and get something happening. As a small business owner, chances are you will need to write for your business at some stage.

Keep in mind that none of us write the perfect words on the first try. Even us copywriters do not sit down and type out perfectly prosed copy on our first attempt. Sometimes, we might get close. But most of the time, we simply start by writing *something* – anything, in fact.

Much of the time the trick is to simply start somewhere.

Even if you spit out the most ridiculous jumble of words there ever was, your aim when starting a piece of writing is to simply get every single thought and word out of your brain and onto the page. Because once you have something, you have something to work with.

Words on a page can be edited, refined, reworked or rejigged – until suddenly, your writing *does* make sense.

Let's look at how a copywriter like me might approach a writing task.

Step 1: Organise Your Page and Content

Starting with a blank document on your computer is often intimidating, right?

To combat this, you might make yourself a bit of a template (or ask for one of mine!).

Start by writing a basic topic at the top of the page (or title if you already have one). Then jot down some potential sub-headings or dot points around what you want to cover in your piece. Add an introduction at the top and a conclusion at the bottom. Easy peasy!

That is literally what I did to start writing this very chapter.

While sometimes yes, I can pick a topic and just blurt it all out on the page from start to finish (gotta love it when that happens!) – much of the time I need to plan it out first.

So, you need:

- Topic or title
- Introduction
- Sub-sections (could be anywhere between three and ten pieces of information you want to cover)
- Conclusion

This might seem like a very basic format – and it is – but it will help you write just about anything, from social media posts, blog posts, news articles, website pages, product descriptions, landing pages and more.

In some instances, while you may indeed use "Introduction" and "Conclusion" as headings, you do not necessarily need to have them in there. Those two are just a guide to help you.

Step 2: Produce a Skeleton Draft

In a skeleton draft, you take your sub-sections or sub-headings and jot down as many facts, figures and thoughts about each aspect.

Here, we are all about the dot points. They can be as garbled as they need to be. They can be two or ten words. It does not matter.

Now you might have:

Topic or title

Introduction

- Explanation about the topic and why it's important.

Sub-Heading 1

- Fact 1
- Fact 2
- Fact 3

Sub-Heading 2

- Fact 1
- Fact 2
- Fact 3

Sub-Heading 3

- Fact 1
- Fact 2
- Fact 3

Conclusion

- Wrap up the topic, main points and conclude with a strong statement.
- You might also include a call to action or an offer here.

Step 3: Write a Rough First Draft

Now that you have planned out your topic and sections and organised some facts or thoughts under each one, you are ready to begin writing.

It is often easier to start with the main body of your content piece by tackling the sub-headings and paragraphs first, and then followed by writing the introduction and conclusion at the end.

Take the first dot point under the first sub-heading, and turn it into a sentence or a paragraph, depending on how much detail you think you need. Then take the second dot point, and again, turn it into a sentence or a paragraph.

Keeping in mind, that when writing digital copy or content, it is best to keep your sentences short and your paragraphs shorter. Once sentence can form an entire paragraph.

It is best to not exceed more than two or three sentences for a paragraph (this may go against what you learnt at school for formal writing, but the idea with digital content is that it is engaging and conversational, while being easy to scan through).

Once you have expanded all your dot points, you've hopefully got something that looks a little like a first draft.

Do not worry if it seems too rough though, as that is what the next step is for – editing.

Step 4: Review, Rewrite and Refine for Second and Third Drafts

Believe it or not, the best writing does not always happen until the second or third drafts.

When you finish the first draft, there is a good chance that it will be fairly wonky. It will need some firm editing and refinement.

Keep in mind that giving your brain a rest between writing the first draft and editing into the second and third drafts can enhance your results dramatically.

Copywriters often give themselves a day or two of breathing space when writing for clients, because ideas tend to percolate in our brains and appear literally overnight. The old saying "sleep on it" is *very* relevant here.

Always edit with a fresh mind where possible, as you are more likely to pick up on things that need adjusting.

If you are still struggling though – it may help to send your copy to a friend to read. Often, someone that is that little bit further away from the topic can really give you good insights as to where you need to refine things.

Read through and fix any glaring issues you can find, and eventually, you will end up with a solid piece of writing.

If you do not have the capacity, send it to a professional copywriter or editor. Often, paying for editing is cheaper than getting someone to write from scratch – and a pro can really add the engaging spice and sparkle that you need for your marketing.

Step 5: Final Proofread

Finally, you need to give your piece the final once over to make sure there are no glaring spelling or grammar mistakes. Again, send it to a friend, your mum, your husband/wife or even older kids. Fresh eyes on the page are the bomb!

Once you have it proofread, you are ready to hit the publish button and share your written masterpiece with the world.

You Made It

I hope that this chapter has given you more insights and more confidence when it comes to your business writing. I firmly believe that a lot of business owners can drastically improve their own writing skills, and in doing so, will end up seeing more success because of it.

You may have heard this before, but the biggest and best copywriting trick is to simply write how you speak. That is exactly what I have done for this entire chapter. I explained my thoughts on this subject just as I would have if you were talking to me in person.

And even if you do end up outsourcing some or all of your copywriting, it helps to understand the principles behind effective copy. This will ensure that anyone you engage with is able to do this for you effectively and get you the results you need.

This leads me to my final piece of advice.

If you follow all my steps to copywriting success and you still feel that you suck at writing, even after several months of practising, it is a call for your business to outsource to a professional.

Of course, yes, I am a copywriter and I would say that, or I wouldn't have a business. *Ha!*

Being able to communicate the right things in the right way to your audience so that you can bring in the clients and customers you need (and therefore that all important cash) is worth doing well.

An experienced copywriter, particularly an experienced search engine optimisation (SEO) copywriter, can approach your copy from both a customer and conversion (sales) perspective and from an SEO perspective, whether it is your website's copywriting, blog posts or sales pages.

And we are masters of being writing "chameleons". We can expertly adjust our tone of voice to match yours, or to create an entirely new one just for you.

In fact, the thing I love doing most as a copywriter is being able to download all those crazy, confusing, jumbled up thoughts from inside your head, make sense of them and turn that crazy jumble into beautiful, edgy, purposeful, strategic and perfect copy that really hits the mark with your customers.

The goal is for you, my lovely business owner, to have that all important confidence in your message and in your brand. You will also end up with far more clarity around who you are and the value that you offer. This will help your business not just survive but truly thrive.

For all those pesky social media posts and emails that you just must write, just give it a go. People do not expect the perfection that you might think that they expect. In fact, perfect can be a real turnoff in a world where consumers now tend to value authenticity and true connection far more.

It is alright to start somewhere and improve over time.

You just need to start.

So, go write something. Write – right now, in fact.

And let me know how you go.

About the Author

Sarah Walkerden, The Rural Copywriter, is a digital marketing messaging and strategy ace. She helps rural and regional businesses win scores of adoring customers and boost their Google rankings.

Her 'no fluff, no bull-dust' approach creates straight-shooting SEO Website Copy that cultivates real results, helping 'agri' and other rural businesses to flourish.

A country girl at heart, Sarah spent years managing websites for large corporate companies in Melbourne. Now she's settled on her rural property in regional Victoria with her young family, her horses and her thriving business.

I've never wanted to lead a 'normal' life. I've always wanted to live a life of freedom, flexibility and fun. To not be tied down to a 9 – 5 job. And to have more impact on the world.

Together, with my husband, we're creating the life WE want to lead. Our kids have the freedom and the space to run, explore and learn about nature and farming. We actively seek out fun and adventure, alongside our business pursuits. And we believe the best is yet to come.

Recently, my husband Toby Billing and I, have taken things one step further and started our own Digital Agency – The Rural Marketing Company.

Finally, I'll leave you with my business vision and mission. It's why I do what I do.

Vision

- To help rural businesses thrive, regardless of location.
- To support the future of Australian Agriculture.
- To support rural and remote communities.
- To empower rural business leaders to chase their wildest dreams and build a life of freedom, flexibility and fun for themselves and their families, from anywhere they so choose.

Sarah Walkerden

The Rural Copywriter

Website: https://www.theruralcopywriter.com.au Facebook: www.facebook.com/theruralcopywriter

The Rural Marketing Company

Website:

https://www.theruralmarketingco.com.au
Facebook: www.facebook.com/theruralmarketingco

Chapter Twelve
Insights From a Start-Up: My First Year in Business

By Phillipa Lawson
Pinnaroo Farms

Introduction

I spent my early twenties going to university, trying numerous jobs, travelling and experiencing life. It was not until my late twenties that life became more serious quite quickly as I experienced two life-changing events. These events gave me a push to pursue the things that I wanted to do.

I had a passion for teaching and decided to get my middle school teaching degree. Then in my early thirties, my husband and I moved back to the family farm. With two small children in tow, we took over the business from my dad.

My husband and I had only just taken over my family's farming business when our region experienced two challenging years of limited rain and severe frost. Our yields were not great, and our lentils did not meet the rigorous visual specifications of the export market. In addition to this, our bottom line was greatly impacted by international export tariffs.

Ultimately, we were left with lentils that we could not sell. Despite their slightly damaged visual appearance, the lentils were still perfectly edible and retained all of their fantastic nutritional value.

On the home front, we had a daughter who was a very fussy eater, which was affecting her sleeping habits. As most parents could tell you, when your child is not sleeping, you will try just about anything that might help!

We were advised to look at our diets and try to increase her protein intake, yet she hated the texture of meat.

Here, my friends, our most ambitious idea was born.

We decided to mill our highly nutritious "non-export-quality" lentils into a gluten-free fine flour that is versatile and a good source of protein and fibre.

And so, we launched our brand Pinnaroo Farms and our amazing first product – red lentil flour! Currently, we are at the very beginning phase of our value-add business.

Taking our less-than-perfect lentils from a potential waste product and turning them into something much more valuable has been a steep learning curve. However, it is certainly helping to make our farming business more sustainable and profitable.

And, yes, our two girls eat it as our red lentil flour can be easily mixed into a lot of yummy tasting foods, thereby significantly increasing protein and nutrition levels in our family's meals and snacks.

My name is Pip, and I'm a fourth generation broadacre farmer in Pinnaroo, South Australia.

I hope you enjoy some of my insights from our first year of business.

Starting With No Guidebook

Navigating a New Industry: Connecting Agriculture and a Value-Add Food

"You are doing what? Is lentil flour even a thing? I never eat lentils. Sounds like a lot of work! What if it fails? We wish you all the best." These were some typical reactions I initially got when my husband and I launched our new business.

Trouble was, while we believed that we had a great idea, there was no guidebook. we had no clue where to start.

Primary producers are integral to the food industry. However, it soon became apparent just how differently the agriculture and food industries operated.

As farmers, we typically do not know our end user. Therefore, I spent months researching, interviewing and listening to people, trying to discover what their pain points were around eating, what were they currently frustrated with in regard to food and nutrition, how do they tend to make a purchase decision and what is important to them while shopping.

I discovered that there was a huge support for Australian producers and especially as Covid-19 was changing the way we ate and behaved. I discovered that people wanted to get back to the basics and convenience, and they wanted Australian grown food.

I spent hours on the internet reading papers on food trends, scientific reports on plant-based proteins and who our potential competitors might be.

Learning about the food industry for me was like turning up to a new job where you do not know anyone, and no one has given you an induction manual!

It was not an easy task. I allocated two to three hours a day to conduct research and interviews. I knew that I needed to educate myself quickly if I was going to make this unique new business work.

If you ever find yourself in a similar position, all I can say is research, research, research.

The Importance of a Vision

Having a vision is important. You need to know why you want to start your business in the first place and what contribution you are trying to make to the world around you. Plus, you also need to learn to be alright with setbacks, failures and changes of plan. Flexibility in your approach, while sticking to your big picture vision, is a must.

My vision was quite simple in the beginning and has since developed the more I have learnt about the food industry. However, this took time to form. I read books, attended free webinars and participated in courses – all of which kept forcing me back to working on this magical "vision".

An important question that I had to ask myself was, "What is my business trying to contribute?"

So, I got to work and, to be honest, it took me nearly a year to formulate my "why" into a few sentences. It is not easy to take all your complex and detailed thoughts and plans around your business and distil it all down into a short, succinct statement.

Mine is still not perfectly worded, but having something defined has helped give me that firm motivation I needed – something tangible that was meaningful to reach for.

This in turn has helped me when I needed to pitch our business idea to others and apply for grant applications. As a bonus, I also read it when I have tough days and feel unmotivated.

My First Five Actions

Right, I have an idea, I know why I am doing this, what is next?

Firstly, I researched what accreditations was required for our food business. I then looked for industry support. I managed to win a grant through Farmers to Founders, a program which guided me through the first three months of our business and ended up providing invaluable support.

As mentioned previously, I conducted extensive customer research, which was (and still is) paramount. Finally, I found a mentor who had business experiences and capabilities that I did not. I was able to learn from their industry insights.

These few simple starting steps had me well on the way towards the beginnings of a successful business.

To Post or Not to Post: The Joys of Self-Promotion

Self-Promotion In the Country

Good old self-promotion, hey? It certainly does not come naturally to me.

I was bought up in a household where self-promotion was not attractive nor deemed necessary. It is a common feeling that "country people" should be humble and not brag. Sound familiar? It is perhaps even worse for us women.

However, now it is expected for all businesses to be on social media all the time and for business owners to be visible.

I find this a challenging aspect of our business. I am a relatively private person and to promote myself and our business in our small country town was hard for me. Being vulnerable, getting in front of the camera and thinking what to say is tricky.

In the beginning, I tried to do a fifteen-second video once a week. Even then I found myself cringing when I went to the local footy match. I had all these overwhelming thoughts, am I posting too much, are people sick of me, do they talk about me?

Frequently listening to marketing podcasts and six months later, I started to accept the idea of self-promotion. I learnt that if I do not tell people about our flour, we will not make many sales. I just had to champion my own brand.

Over time, I am slowly becoming more comfortable with self-promotion. I know our lentil flour will not be for everyone, but it will be for those who need it. I feel that it is important to come to terms with this in business, as we may not be for everyone nor will we be liked by everyone. We need to define and know our perfect target audience and focus our attention on serving them.

You will cop some criticism here and there, but those who do criticise are not your ideal customer, so it does not matter.

In saying all of this, I still get nervous putting videos up of myself!

Testing One, Two, Three, Is Anyone Listening?

Have I had social media posts that have flopped, had no engagement or posts that have sounded too salesy? Yep! I have also lost followers on social media and have no idea why.

The amount of free social media marketing advice available to you is great. However, it is similar to when you have your first baby. You are bombarded with every idea, suggestion and opinion under the sun. It is about navigating your way through all of the noisy marketing advice and finding what works for you and your business.

I started with a very basic strategy when it came to posting. Most of my posts were (and still are) based around four themes that our customers were interested in or could relate to.

How did I work all this out? Trial, error, posting frequently and analysing which content created engagement. This took me a good six months! I had to learn who my customers were and how they responded.

I still run tests from time to time to check if my customer assumptions remain accurate.

Keep Moving: The Power of One

This was probably one of the best pieces of advice that someone gave me. "Pip, just do one thing daily to keep your business moving forward."

The start-up phase of small business is a roller coaster. Even when I felt absolutely swamped, had sick kids or when we were busy on the farm, I have always done one thing every day for our business.

Whether it was answering an email, replying to direct messages, making a phone call or creating a social media post, as long as it was something, that is something I achieved.

I have also focused all my energy on one social media platform. This will change as the business grows. However, for me to manage our marketing, I had to choose one to start with, to help me avoid being overwhelmed.

Trials and Tribulations of Mindset

Dealing With Burnout and Work-Life Balance

This by far has been the most challenging part of starting our business. I am still trying to manage and achieve the right work-life balance, and some weeks I get it right and other weeks I do not.

During our first year of business, I was working ten-hour days, six days a week. This ultimately (and obviously) was quite ridiculous and definitely not sustainable. I felt the pressure to be on top of everything, and because we were entering into a new industry, I needed to know exactly how it worked.

My exercise went out the window and I was getting sore neck and shoulders from intensely staring at a computer screen. However, I am my own worst enemy as I am not very good at switching off.

In February 2021, I could feel myself burning out and began questioning, "Why am I doing this?"

I began to listen to helpful podcasts and discovered Janine Allis' podcast *Superwomen … We Ain't*. She stated a few home truths, and I began to follow her advice and reign in my chaotic ways! I made exercise a priority and started to look at ways to get off the farm. I also write lists (as I am a list girl) at the beginning of the week to help me stay focused.

One Sunday morning, I woke up at 5 am to do the farm book work. Yes, I'm a morning person and find that I can get a lot achieved before the household awakes! My daughter came in at 7:30 am and wanted me to colour with her. I told her, "No, honey, I have to do another hour on the business and then I will colour with you."

She stormed out yelling, "I hate your business and you never play with us ever." Kids, they are so perceptive and honest.

Up until then, my kids never really said anything to me about all the hours I was spending pouring over the computer screen. I am so thankful for her outburst as she was right.

Is there a balance between work and life? I believe that there is not a balance as such, but some weeks are more harmonious than others and that is just the way it is.

As the months have rolled on, I have decided to put restrictions on my time. I try not to do any business after school pick-up, at least until the kids go to bed. That way I know that I am present with my kids, which keeps all of us happy.

Abundance Mindset

Over the last two years, I have been working on my mindset. When my husband and I went through some tough seasons together, we decided that the only thing we did have control over was the way we thought. From that experience, being genuinely happy for others' successes or wins, and trying not to dwell on the negatives, have provided us with a sense of freedom.

However, this mindset can be tricky to maintain while on social media. I have to catch myself when I start to compare and judge what competitors are doing. However, I remind myself that I do not know what their business structure, finances, cost of goods and marketing is like. So, how can I possibly compare my business with theirs?

I have found that our business flows better when we stay in our own lane and focus on what we do best. Sure, we keep the occasional eye on competitors, but we do not get wrapped up in that dark trap of comparison.

Conclusion

I hope some of my insights into the first year of our business has been useful or even helpful! I definitely do not have all the answers, nor have I figured it all out.

Whenever I start to feel burnt out or have difficulty focusing, I remember how our business will positively contribute to our local region, industry and our customers.

I also strongly believe in doing one thing each day to keep your business in momentum. This mentality has allowed me a peace of mind when I have had sick kids at home or when I am needed to help on the farm. Balancing our work, life and community commitments is challenging. Listen to your inner self or gut feeling and just go for it!

Start that idea, post that Facebook video of yourself, you may not be everyone's cup of tea, but that is alright.

Give it a red hot go and see what happens.

Good luck!

About the Author

Pip likes long walks on the riverbank sipping pinacolatos...

...while that sounds great, it doesn't happen that often!

In reality, Pip is a mother of two and along with her husband, they manage their broadacre farm, located in Pinnaroo, South Australia.

They're currently in the midst of launching their sprouted lentil flour, which is their new value-add business!

Prior to this, Pip did a degree in Environmental Management and Tourism, and did her Diploma of Education in middle school. In between studding at university, Pip spent a year overseas working and travelling and then came back to Australia and worked in many different places, with Fraser Island being one of her favourites.

As an outdoor type of person and garden enthusiast, this sees Pip trying to avoid inside duties ...mainly housework! While the office work does regularly call her, Pip will sometimes drive into the middle of a paddock just to check the crops and answer emails.

On a serious note, Pip is very passionate about her family, the future of Australian agriculture, soil conservation, creating a nutritious ingredient, growing a sustainable business and her small community of Pinnaroo.

www.pinnaroofarms.com.au

Chapter Thirteen
Digital Marketing Essentials for Rural Businesses

By Sarah Walkerden
The Rural Copywriter / The Rural Marketing Company

Digital marketing can be a bit of a minefield.

As modern businesses, we know that it's essential for us to make the most of all the digital marketing avenues that are available. Yet, it's not always easy to figure out the how, what, when or where.

The sheer number of choices can feel overwhelming. It's tricky to know which ones will work best for you or what to focus on first.

In this chapter, I can give you the low-down on how the digital marketing landscape works, what's on offer, and where you should be starting. As a digital marketing specialist, I'm all about keeping things simple, achievable and smart.

We do this by laying solid foundations first. Just like how you might do when building a house or a farm shed. You want your shed to weather all those storms and stay upright, no matter what gets thrown in its way!

Hence, the quality end results we're looking for relies on getting those critical foundations right, before embarking on anything more complicated and trying to spread ourselves too thin, over too much, too soon.

We can follow a step-by-step process, which certainly helps prevent you from feeling overwhelmed. That way, your business is not just set up to survive, but to thrive, no matter what gets thrown your way. If you skip crucial steps and neglect your foundations, it's all just going to fall apart.

Let's look at what every rural business needs to succeed online.

Handy Beginner Marketing Lingo

Tactics Versus Strategy

Let's begin with a basic understanding of the difference between a marketing "tactic" and a marketing "strategy".

A tactic is a specific marketing activity that you do.

A strategy is a long-term plan to achieve a specific goal.

In many cases, you can have both a tactic and a strategy in one. For example, search engine optimisation (SEO) is both a tactic that you do and has an overarching strategy. Your SEO strategy comes under your broader marketing strategy.

It's always important to ensure that you set a holistic and cohesive strategy that governs your individual strategies and tactics. This ensures that all the marketing activities you undertake contribute to the larger or overall goal.

Organic Versus Paid Tactics

Next, it's also important to understand the differences between organic strategies and tactics and paid strategies and tactics.

Organic marketing tactics are generally free. They drive traffic to your website or landing pages for free, for example, SEO, social media posts and content marketing.

Paid marketing tactics are generally paid social media ads or Google ads. You're paying for the traffic and paying for that sale.

Successful business marketing ideally uses both. However, I always recommend that you begin with organic strategies first as this allows you to get your foundation (website design, messaging, etc) right before spending further money on ads.

If your website looks or reads terribly, it just isn't going to work. No amount of paid traffic is going to fix that. Also, many of us are limited by budget in the early days of business so you'll want to take advantage of as much organic marketing as you possibly can in the beginning.

Hence, we're going to focus on organic methods in this chapter.

The Aim of Marketing

For most businesses who trade online, you want to focus on three main steps.

1. Build and optimise your website.
2. Send traffic to your website – through your chosen tactics (social media, SEO, paid ads, etc).
3. Get conversions – in the form of sales, bookings or enquiries.

It sounds simple (and it is!), but if you've been in business even just a little while, you'll know that it's not that easy. When everything starts to feel overwhelming, it's useful to bring yourself back to these three steps.

There's a good chance that you'll be able to diagnose any problems, by figuring out which one you're struggling with.

Is it a website problem? Is it a traffic problem? Or is it a conversion problem (which can also be related to the website problem)?

The other big thing to ask yourself when things aren't going the way you thought they would is whether you're being customer-focused *enough*.

Marketing is never about us as a business, no matter how much you might feel like it is. It's never about us. It's about your customers.

Every piece of marketing material and every activity you do within your business should always be focused on your target audience and your ideal customer. If something isn't working, there's a good chance that you either don't know your customer well enough or that your marketing has missed the mark in serving them somewhere along the line.

It Starts With a Great Website

Your website is one of the most important aspects of your marketing. Some marketing folks might disagree, with the rise of social media. And yes, you can potentially build and run a successful business using social media alone. Yet, I don't recommend it.

Having a great website is basically giving your business an online home or base camp. It gives your customers a reference point and a solid place for them to come and interact.

It's also yours! Relying on social media is tricky, as you don't own the platform. Things can, and do, change drastically overnight when platforms make changes to their algorithms and how they want things to work. Leaving us as business owners on shaky, unpredictable ground.

Quite frankly, customers take you more seriously when you have a great-looking, easy-to-use website.

Build and Design

First up, you clearly need to *build* your website.

I recommend for you to use Wordpress, or if you need something a bit quicker and simpler for an e-commerce website, go with either BigCommerce or Shopify.

Wordpress is ideal as it gives you complete flexibility as you can plug in any functionality you may need now, or into the future. It will grow with you. Plus, you own everything!

BigCommerce is great for powerful, easy-to-manage e-commerce websites. Shopify is also popular but a little more complex. Keep in mind that these platforms own your website. If you want to move your website design in future, you'll be starting the process from scratch.

When using Wordpress, you'll also need a hosting company. I recommend either Siteground or VentraIP (Aussie-based). BigCommerce and Shopify are fully hosted, so you don't need a third-party host.

The next thing to know, that is while Wordpress is free to use, you'll want to use a page-building software that comes with templates to build your website more easily.

The two I use are Avada and Divi. Avada is my favourite as they have some great templates and powerful features. Divi is easier to use; however, I can pick a Divi site from a mile away, regardless of customisation, as they all look similar.

If you're not tech-savvy when it comes to building websites, or you simply don't have an eye for design, I don't recommend you trying to build your website yourself. Hire a professional, please!

It doesn't need to be expensive, and you'll get a far more sophisticated result. If you can, avoid cheap overseas providers! There's really nothing worse than visiting a website that's clunky, looks like a backyard job and is impossible to use.

Copywriting

I come across many business websites that have terrible copywriting. They often spend thousands on a beautiful website design, but then throw a whole heap of rubbish words up on the site that often doesn't make any sense.

Yes, professional copywriting is an extra expense, but it does determine how successful your website will be. It also determines how successful your entire business will be. Unless you can clearly communicate your value to the right people, nothing in your business is going to work.

The right website messaging doesn't just assist your website, it can also help to determine your overall marketing messaging and tone of voice.

You'll find that investing in website copywriting will allow you to use that same messaging on your socials, in your blog posts, on any printed marketing material and even while you're chatting to a potential customer on the phone. Trust me when I say that it's worth getting right.

Copywriting is such a massive topic (which I've even covered in a separate chapter), but here are a few golden rules:

- It's about your customer and how you solve their problems – not about you. Don't just describe what you do. Paint a picture in words as to what you can do for them.
- Your copy should be outcome focused.
- Emotions sell, facts justify.

Search Engine Optimisation

I've included SEO here as a separate item because it's one of the most misunderstood marketing tactics. There are a lot of "turkeys" and "cowboys" in the industry who just love to bamboozle business owners with a heap of crazy promises and technical jargon, but then they don't deliver.

SEO is something that needs to be weaved into your website. It has both a website technical and design component *and* a copywriting component. It's also a standalone tactic or strategy. This is where it gets complicated.

I've included SEO under the website section, as it's a much better idea to make your website SEO-friendly from the get-go.

Here's your basic overview of the different moving parts of a successful SEO strategy:

- Keyword research – to accurately determine what words and phrases are best for you to target.
- Technical SEO – to optimise your website to load as quickly as possible, optimising for mobile viewing and other such things.
- Copywriting SEO – to engage with your customers and attract Google.
- Ongoing quality content – adding regular high-value content, such as blog posts.
- Quality backlinks – getting other reputable websites to link to your website.

The great news here, and one of my best tricks to making your initial investment around your website go further, is that you can tick off the first three aspects of SEO while also tackling your website and copywriting to engage with your customers.

Firstly, get some keyword research performed (a relatively minor expense that's often under $500).

Then, get your website designed and built using SEO best practice. Most website-building templates will give you a great foundation for SEO as they will already be optimised, but you may need a professional developer to ensure that everything is implemented in the best possible way for best results.

Finally, engage a professional for your copywriting needs, someone who can write for your customers *and* for Google. This is called SEO website copywriting (something I specialise in) It is a very strategic and delicate artform to keep the balance right between customers and SEO.

Content and Social Media Marketing

When we're talking about "content", we're referring to blog posts and social media content (which you also might send out to your email database). Content marketing is a critical element to your success as a rural business owner.

No one really appreciates being sold to these days. The idea of content marketing is to inspire, educate and entertain your target audience as a way of building goodwill between you and your business, and your ideal customers.

The golden rule is help first, sell later. Use the rule of 80% value and 20% sales.

Content can take many different forms, including written content, video, audio and images. You can place this content on your website and across many different social media platforms. The platforms and form you choose is determined by your goals and where your audience hangs out and engages the most.

This means that you may have to do some market and audience research to ensure that you are visible in the right places. At the very least, make sure you have a business page on Facebook as this is the most widely used platform across the world.

Next, you might consider Instagram, LinkedIn, YouTube, Pinterest and TikTok.

As with most marketing, these choices come down to your preferences and some experimentation to gauge what will work and what won't. Start by focusing on just one or two platforms. Get them going and then gradually add new ones in if and when you need to.

Start With a Simple Content Marketing Plan

The main goal of your content is to offer value to your audience that encourages goodwill and engagement so that they get to know you and hopefully buy from you.

A scattergun approach is haphazard. A consistent plan and execution are always your best bet.

When starting out, here's a few plans I recommend that you can choose from:

Plan 1

- Weekly detailed written blog post/podcast/video – post a link to the full version on Monday
- Tuesday until Friday – take snippets or quotes out of your longer Monday post, for your socials

Plan 2

- Monday – written blog post
- Tuesday – quote from blog post
- Wednesday – quick Facebook Live recapping topic or pulling out a main element from the blog post

- Thursday – case study or testimonial from a client who has achieved what you're talking about

- Friday – something more light-hearted or personal that might be related to the weekly topic

Plan 3

- Monday – blog/video/podcast

- Wednesday – quote

- Friday – case study

- Leave Tuesdays and Thursdays for more fun, ad hoc content.

As you can see, the options are limitless. You may well need to implement something like this for a month or two, to get a feel for whether or not it's working for you and your audience. There are many other options such as Facebook Stories, Instagram Stories and Reels, etc.

The golden rule is: Keep it simple and consistent. Start small and build more sophistication over time.

If you struggle with time, you could schedule posts in advance via a scheduler. Spend one day per month to write your main blog posts or produce your videos ahead of time. Roll them out automatically over the course of the month.

Play to your strengths where possible – at least to start with! If you love speaking and engaging with people, record a video. If you prefer to write, share a written post.

Basic Lead Generation and Sales Funnels

Finally, you want to implement a basic lead generation and sales funnel to build your email marketing database and bring in a consistent flow of customers.

Here's the gist:

1. Offer freebie/lead magnet

You offer your audience something for free of high value that they desire and that solves a specific problem for them – think a checklist, e-book, quiz, etc.

For them to gain access to this amazing free item, they must provide their email address, which then puts them on your database.

This process must be done with full transparency as there are legalities around how you can collect and use their information. Make sure you have links to your privacy policy on your signup form and along with a General Data Protection Regulation disclaimer.

2. Send Freebie and Five to Ten Nurture Emails

Once a potential client or customer is on your database, send them the freebie, and then send them an automated series of nurture emails, which gradually drip-feed them content designed to help them get to know you and what you offer.

3. Encourage them to check out your sales page within each email.

You can then send them to a sales page to encourage them to buy a product or book a service.

Even if they don't buy after receiving the nurture emails, they can go onto your general email marketing list, and you can continue to email them and nurture them over time.

This is the basics. You can make this process a lot more sophisticated by adding steps and using a low-cost product and gradually upselling to them or offering the high-cost product. If they say no, you can still offer them a lower-cost product.

To start, you want to build your database so that you can continually touch base with them and remind them of your presence – as long as you do this mindfully and carefully! You don't want to bombard them with a tonne of sales messages because there's a good chance that they will unsubscribe.

Keep offering value in the form of free tips and advice.

Moving on to the Advanced Aspects

After you have your website, content and social media sorted and a basic sales funnel in place, you need to keep testing, monitoring and adjusting them over time.

Now, it's time to move on to more advanced tactics, such as paid ads (on social media and Google), more technical and advanced SEO, guest blogging, podcasts (starting your own and/or appearing on others), publishing books and seeking out public relations (feature articles in newspapers or magazines).

When choosing what to do next, keep in mind that different marketing activities have different aims. Paid ads are designed to reach more people and attract more immediate sales.

Submitting guest blog posts to larger industry websites, appearing as a guest on a podcast, or writing and publishing a book (or ten!) is more about positioning yourself as a leader and an authority in your space *and* driving more organic traffic to your website or social media.

Always think about the end goal that you want a piece of marketing or a marketing tactic to achieve.

Think strategically and think smart. Play to your strengths and seek out the opportunities in your industry to get in front of the right people and establish your credibility.

Conclusion

If you take anything away from this, it's to build a solid foundation to help the sexier, more advanced tactics work.

Many business owners look for shortcuts in the form of paid advertising, but ads don't convert if you're not clear on who you are and can convey that on your website and social media.

You could have the greatest ad in the whole wide world that gets heaps of clicks, but if people click through to a crappy, unclear website, they're not going to buy.

Business owners think that a Facebook ad for instance can merely contain a pretty picture and the words "buy from us because we're great", and they expect that to work. People need to feel something significant in order to stop scrolling and take notice. Therefore, you'll want to tap right into their emotional needs and desires first and foremost to grab their attention.

Marketing can be simple, but it also needs to be strategic and clever. Your job as a clever business owner is to shake people out of their daydreaming and mindless scrolling.

Cut right through that noise and inspire them to take action.

The biggest piece of advice I can give you is to be authentic and real. The more you can let your unique personality shine through into your branding and marketing, the more people are likely to connect with you and want to buy or work with you.

Authenticity is everything right now in such a noisy, crazy world.

Get real. Get your foundations in place. Progress to advanced tactics when you can. Keep building those marketing blocks higher in a sustainable way.

And always, be you.

Part 4

Systems for Growth

Chapter Fourteen
Bookkeeping to Grow Your Business

By Emily Sinderberry
EJS Business Services

Introduction

Bookkeeping, love it or hate it, it's an essential component of business.

I am Emily Sinderberry, the founder of EJS Business Services. I am a passionate rural bookkeeper and registered Business Activity Statement (BAS) agent living on a farm ninety kilometres north of Condobolin in Central West, New South Wales.

I support rural, regional and remote businesses to better understand their numbers, streamline business systems and drive growth in business. I do this through the provision of strategic bookkeeping and BAS services, accounting software setup and training, and business strategy coaching.

In this chapter, you will gain a better understanding about bookkeeping and how you can use it to grow your business. You will learn what bookkeeping is, technologies to assist you, systemisation and efficiencies, outsourcing your bookkeeping, and how to better understand your numbers and monitoring your business. Let's dive in!

What Is Bookkeeping?

Bookkeeping is systematically recording and organising the financial activities of a business.

It involves the process of recording, analysing and interpreting the financial transactions associated with the business. There are two foundational tasks in small business bookkeeping: data entry and bank reconciliation. Without these, other bookkeeping tasks cannot happen. Each financial transaction is recorded based on supporting documentation.

Bookkeeping differs from accounting because the accounting process uses the books kept by the bookkeeper (or the business owner), to prepare the end of year financial statements and tax returns to comply with the taxation laws.

Bookkeeping Basics

A major fundamental in business is the use of a cash or accrual accounting system. If you are using cash accounting, you record your transaction when cash changes hands. Using accrual accounting, you record purchases or sales immediately when they happen even if the cash does not change hands until a later time.

Effective bookkeeping requires an understanding of the business's basic accounts/categories and their sub accounts that make up the business's chart of accounts. The chart of accounts is a full list of accounts used in the business to categorise financial transactions.

The main categories are revenue, expenses, assets, liabilities and equity. The sub accounts have more specific categories such as sales, advertising, bank fees, loans, plant and equipment, etc. The revenue and expenses make up the profit and loss statement. The assets, liabilities and equity are the accounts that compose the business's balance sheet.

The accounting equation is:

Equity = Assets - Liabilities

This equation is the foundation of the double entry bookkeeping system, and it represents the relationship between the assets, liabilities and owner's equity of a business.

Assets are the things the business owns such as its inventory, accounts receivable, fixed assets (such as plant, equipment, land and vehicles).

Liabilities are what the company owes such as what they owe to suppliers, banks and business loans, mortgages and other debt.

Equity is the investment a business owner and any other investors have in the business. It also includes money introduced or withdrawn by the owners or shareholders.

General Ledger or Accounts

"The Books"

Assets	Liabilities	Owner Equity	Income	Expenses
(Things Owned)	(Things Owed)	(Money from owner)	(Money In)	(Money Out)

Assets, Liabilities, and Owner Equity flow down into the Balance Sheet.

Income and Expenses flow down into the Profit & Loss (P&L).

The five accounts that make up a general ledger, and how they flow down into the main accounting reports.

What Is Involved in Bookkeeping?

Standard bookkeeping includes processing purchases, sales, receipts and payments, processing payroll and maintaining entitlements and employee records, bank reconciliation, providing reports for preparation of BAS, producing reports for both management and the business accountant, and record keeping.

Technologies to Assist You

Accounting Software

There are many different accounting software options on the market today, and it can be difficult to decide what is best for your business.

The most common accounting software systems for small businesses are Xero, MYOB, QuickBooks Online and Phoenix by AgData (which is a rural-focused software). You should consider price, features, how it integrates with other systems in your business, and ease of access to support.

Accounting Software Add-ons

With the advancement of cloud accounting software, there are many add-ons available that link to your accounting software programme. For example, Xero has a marketplace of apps that integrate with Xero for various industries.

Software companies no longer need to develop a whole system to cater for everyone as there are lots of different add-ons in the market that can be integrated to the accounting software for a specific business. However, adding on additional apps often means that there are other significant costs involved.

Common add-on software that I see for businesses using Xero is the use of Hubdoc, which is a free document processing system. Some businesses also use Dext (formally Receipt Bank); however, this comes with extra costs. There are payroll add-ons such as Deputy, which can help with timesheet, and leave and award management.

For rural businesses, Xero also has an add-on app called Figured, which is a livestock, crop and production tracking, farm budgeting and forecasting tool.

More Apps to Help Build Your Business

Various other apps can be added to your tech stack to help your business. Your tech stack is the combination of software programs and technology that you use to manage and run your business.

Such technologies could include Dropbox or Google Drive (or a document system similar to those), a task or project management system such as Trello, Asana or Monday.com. If you want to connect your apps and automate workflows, you could also consider using Zapier to enhance the workflow and integration between programs.

Bookkeeping Systemisation and Efficiencies

Systems to Integrate

An ideal bookkeeping system would have documents flowing from your emails into a document processing system (such as Hubdoc), and then these documents will flow through to your accounting software so that they are ready to be reconciled against bank transactions or paid if they are outstanding bills.

Timing and Key Activities

The most important part of bookkeeping in a small business is to ensure that it is done regularly to make sure reports are up-to-date and accurate. Hence, key activities such as your BAS can be completed on time each quarter or month.

Deciding What You Need

With so many systems and software available these days, it can be difficult to work out what you need for your business.

I often recommend starting simple with the essential software such as your accounting software. As you become familiar with your accounting software, you can start exploring other add-ons that might make your bookkeeping and office management more efficient and streamlined.

If you are unsure of where to start looking or which apps may help you, reach out to a bookkeeper, your tax agent/accountant or even other business connections.

They can suggest what has worked for them or what they have seen other businesses use to help streamline systems and save time. This can be a low-cost solution to help you find an efficient and profitable system.

Outsourcing and Working with a Bookkeeper Remotely

What Does Outsourcing Bookkeeping Look Like?

A bookkeeper is a "keeper of the books", and they record and organise a business' financial data. It is not just historical processing – it is now an integrated business management system.

Certified bookkeepers have proven that they have performed bookkeeping services to a significant level for a time period and have proven a level of bookkeeping knowledge. They are often members of professional associations, and they may be a registered BAS agent with the Tax Practitioners Board.

When you do your own bookkeeping, you are potentially increasing the risk of problems and mistakes if you are not familiar with bookkeeping. Common DIY bookkeeping issues include:

- Incorrect claiming of GST, resulting in penalties or needing to amend a BAS

- Incorrect or late payment of superannuation, resulting in fines and interest (which can be more than the superannuation amount itself!)

- Ongoing orders, invoices or inventory problems not being resolved

- Employee entitlements not being taken care of correctly

- Inaccurate management reports resulting in an ambiguous picture of your business performance

- Late lodgement of activity statements resulting in interest charges

You can expect a competent bookkeeper to establish and maintain a chart of accounts, manage data entry, complete journals as required, prepare BAS and run management reports. You would also expect them to handle the bulk of the transactions including accounts payable, accounts receivable, payroll, inventory and reconciliation of relevant accounts.

Only registered BAS and tax agents are permitted to advise or help you ascertain your liabilities, obligations or entitlements of the areas of the BAS, which include GST, pay as you go withholding, which is associated with payroll, pay as you go instalment payments, fringe benefits tax payments, wine equalisation tax, fuel tax credits and luxury car tax.

To be a tax or BAS agent, an individual must be fit and proper, have minimum formal qualifications, continue to have sufficient ongoing relevant experience, have an appropriate level of professional indemnity insurance, undergo continuing professional education, and maintain professionalism in accordance with at least a statutory code of conduct.

Adherence with the code of conduct reinforces the concepts of honesty and integrity, independence and confidentiality.

A BAS agent provides services confidently using knowledge and skills to take "reasonable care" to ensure that tax law is applied correctly for the business. A BAS agent, however, will not advise or liaise with the Australian Tax Office on income tax matters (that is the role of a registered tax agent).

A BAS agent is committed to providing expert service and, therefore, I advise that you should engage with a BAS agent where possible to ensure that you're getting the most professional service. You can check if someone is registered as a BAS agent by visiting the Tax Practitioners Board's website and searching the BAS agent register.

How Would I Work With a Remote Bookkeeper?

There are many ways to work with a remote bookkeeper. You can engage a bookkeeper to complete core duties such as data entry, bank reconciliation and monthly reporting.

Additional duties can include accounts receivable (and credit control), accounts payable and payroll. Advanced duties include end-of-year reporting, business strategy, training and virtual office management.

You can get started by outsourcing some core duties to your bookkeeper and then over time ask them to take on more aspects of the bookkeeping for your business.

Every engagement with a remote bookkeeper will feel a little bit different; however, generally the business owner would forward emails with relevant documentation to the bookkeeper for them to attend to, or you may save the documentation to a cloud storage system and then the bookkeeper picks it up from there and processes it accordingly.

Also, you could have a shared email inbox for finance-related information to save time! Have a conversation with a bookkeeper and get a feel for how you could get started and how it could work for your business!

To help your business, a modern bookkeeper will:

- Improve business systems and streamline processes
- Integrate the best technology that is appropriate to automate their process as much as possible
- Manage the technology and the business systems to ensure that they are performing as intended
- Report, validate and provide certainty to the business about what they are doing
- Ensure all compliance requirements are met

Remember though, you are only outsourcing the bookkeeping task and *not* the responsibility! What do I mean by this? You still need to be accountable to monitoring your cashflow, checking in with your bookkeeper and making sure the business finances are sustainable.

How Do I Get Started?

Firstly, I recommend that you ask yourself what tasks the bookkeeper will be required to perform and how long those tasks are likely to take. You also need to consider what level of bookkeeping the business can afford – can you afford to outsource all of the bookkeeping tasks, or can you only outsource part of it?

Once you have decided what you are going to outsource, you can advertise using the internet or asking your tax agent for a referral, or you could keep your eye out for bookkeepers online. A great place to find rural bookkeepers is on The Virtual Cooee HUB (www.thevirtualcooee.com.au).

When you have found some bookkeepers, review them and identify the ones that would be the best fit for your business. Invite them to have a chat about your business and bookkeeping requirements.

You can ask the potential bookkeeper:

- If they have any experience with other businesses in your industry.
- When they are available, what are their working hours, and whether they can work remotely.
- About their business, qualifications, knowledge and experience.
- How long have they been in business, whether they employ others, and if they are a member of a professional association.
- If they have professional indemnity insurance.
- What is their hourly rate or the fixed charges, and how often do they invoice in terms of payment.
- If they have a current client that they could refer as a referee.

Once you have chosen a bookkeeper, they will provide a letter of engagement that you must sign before the engagement can start.

You then provide them with access to your software and any document storage systems that you are using. Finally, make sure that you are both clear on the communication arrangements!

Understanding Your Numbers and Monitoring Your Business

Understanding Key Reports

Key financial reports to understand for your business are the profit and loss, balance sheet and cashflow statement reports.

- **Profit and loss:** A financial report that shows the revenue and expenses for a time period. It also includes the gross profit and net profit amounts. The report demonstrates how profitable the business is.

- **Balance sheet:** A report that breaks down your business' financial situation. It includes the assets, liabilities and equity of the business. Its purpose is to show what your business owes and owns.

- **Cashflow statement:** This report summarises the amount of cash and cash equivalents entering and leaving a business. It measures how well a business manages its cash position.

These reports should be reviewed monthly and compared to a budget to ensure the business is on track to achieving its goals.

What KPIs Should I Track?

Key performance indicators (KPIs) are measurable indicators that show the health of your business and helps track the progress towards business goals. The main financial KPIs to track for your business include gross profit margin and net profit margin.

- **Gross profit margin:** This will tell you how much money is remaining after paying for the product or service that you sold. The higher your gross profit margin, the more money you have remaining to pay for other business expenses such as wages, rent and marketing.

$$\text{Gross Profit Margin} = \frac{(\text{revenue} - \text{cost of goods sold})}{\text{revenue}} \times 100$$

- **Net profit margin:** This is used to measure how profitable your business is and how well your revenue is being used.

$$\text{Net Profit Margin} = \frac{\text{revenue} - \text{total expenses}}{\text{revenue}} \times 100$$

For example:

$$\text{Net Profit Margin} = \frac{100{,}000 - 60{,}000}{100{,}000} \times 100$$

$$= \mathbf{40\%}$$

This means that for every $1 you earn, your business keeps $0.40. If you compare the net profit margin from year-to-year, it will help to see if an increase in revenue increases the profit at the same rate. This allows you to keep track of the business and whether it is continuing to make a profit.

There are various other KPIs that you can track including monthly revenue, quick ratio, customer acquisition cost, lifetime value of a customer, conversion rate, accounts receivable aging and many more! The KPIs that you choose to track should be aligned with your stage of business and business objectives.

Why should you track these KPIs? Tracking KPIs will provide accountability in your business, allow goals to be set and tracked, tell you when something is wrong, and it provides physical proof and value to the business.

How to Make Decisions Based on the Numbers

When checking these indicators, you need to look for changes. For instance, if it is an increase in profit, ask yourself, what did you do right in that period? You may have changed something and can continue with the change to further increase profits.

If the profit decreases, maybe you need to look at what you did differently and consider how you could improve it. Perhaps you spent more money on advertising but did not attract any more revenue.

It is very important to have accurate and timely financial data to ensure that you are making reliable and accurate decisions in your business. Analysing these KPIs can also alert you to errors in data entry.

Conclusion

My final advice for easy but vital bookkeeping practices you should follow: do not leave it to the last minute, keep records nice and tidy, store your supporting documentation online (you can achieve that paperless office that you have been waiting for!), and keep business and personal finances separate.

The key to successful remote bookkeeping relationships is clear and consistent communication. Remember, outsource the task, not the responsibility!

Communication is king!

About the Author

Emily Sinderberry is an experienced bookkeeper, registered BAS agent, farmer, community advocate and virtual assistant, located on a property north of Condobolin in Central West NSW. Emily is the founder of EJS Business Services and is driven by a passion for supporting rural small business. She takes pride in providing outstanding online bookkeeping and other business services to rural, regional and remote businesses.

Emily's goal is to empower business owners to streamline and systemise their office management as well as taking the fear out of their bookkeeping management.

Emily is also the co-founder of The Virtual Cooee which has created an online HUB for businesses to connect with rural and regional virtual assistants and freelancers.

For further information see:

www.ejsbusinessservices.com.au

www.thevirtualcooee.com.au

Chapter Fifteen
The Art of Delegation –
Even When You Don't Want To

By Melanie Fitzgibbon
Camelot Camels & Noosa Camel Rides

Not a delegator? When you would rather die trying to do everything yourself than delegate? Be careful what you wish for!

Delegation is not a sign of weakness but of strength – strength of trust and understanding of your own superpowers. Come on a journey with me and I will tell you why I was once in the "die trying" mode, then forced to change and now celebrate every day that I did so.

Why Am I a Rural Business Woman?

I have two full-time jobs in a coastal rural community, both of which I love. One as a teacher and director of a kindergarten and the other in partnership with my amazing husband at Camelot Camels & Noosa Camel Rides.

As I write this, we are one of a handful of cameleers left providing commercial rides due to Covid-19 and the hefty costs of insurance. I'm also currently on leave from my teaching position.

Our camel rides can be found at agricultural shows, events, festivals and on the beach at Noosa North Shore. Our camels were mostly wild or came with training that needed to be modified for our needs.

Even with Covid-19, we managed to remain one of the last ones standing. I believe that was due to the love and faith my husband and I have for our fury family. From the beginning of 2020, they were my world and solace.

I have always done everything myself. I believed that no one could do what I needed done or how I wanted it done. I'm also an extrovert who gets distracted by better options of what I'm supposed to do.

Having an invite for a coffee catch-up or doing my accounts for business activity statements … well, let's face it, there's no choice here and probably never will be, unless you're an accountant.

This wasn't just the case with business, but at home as well. I would have loved a lovely, clean and tidy house all the time with a garden to match, just like in a magazine. I wanted a picture perfect and lovely cooked meal at a gloriously set table each night with our children. Who was I kidding?

Let's be honest here, this was never going to happen while I remained distracted and overcommitted. I had been overcommitted for ten years. Working seven days a week, always ten hours a day.

I was often so busy being busy, I felt that I was slamming myself from one task to another. I was always late everywhere I went as I was always time poor, overcommitted and easily distracted. I realise that I feel sorrier for my husband now more than ever.

The Wake-up Call of My Diagnosis

In October 2019, at forty-five years old, I started to experience what I thought were hormonal changes. I needed to see my

GP but didn't have time. When Covid-19 broke out in 2020, our business took a real hit.

Also, with being confined to home, I felt that it was going to kill me. The extrovert in me was going to die an isolated death with no audience to watch.

I didn't live alone, my husband and two adult boys were with me. Facetime began to be my only way out. I also enjoyed the indulgence of vodka. I was happy and connected with my friends through Facetime. This was now acceptable.

However, I started to experience what I thought at the time was kidney stones due to the vodka I was merrily drinking. It hurt to breath in. I would have a panic attack if I felt a sneeze coming on, as I knew it was going to hurt.

Since it was crippling my performance during my ten-hour work days, a doctor's appointment was necessary. After various testing over a six-week period, I was told I had stage four ovarian cancer.

I didn't panic at first, I wanted to know what the plan was. How were all these specialists going to save my life so I could get back to being me?

As I completed my first two rounds of chemotherapy, this was when I realised that now was the time to panic. The questions floating through my head were sometimes so loud that I would break out in tears to stop them. Shower crying became a daily occurrence.

This was not a battle I was ready for. What if the chemotherapy didn't work? What if my scheduled surgery wasn't successful? What happens to my family if I didn't survive my scheduled surgery? What if … what if … what if?

My solution was to make sure that the life my husband and I built could carry on for him if I wasn't there. I started to picture myself not around in certain situations and how I could make sure that there was a system in place to provide for him.

What I didn't realise was that these systems were making my life easier. I was now only focusing on the important stuff because that's all I could manage.

As I progressed through my treatment, I knew I was going to make it. I had complete faith in my body's ability to love living. Now that I had trust in others that were doing the things I loathed, it freed me to focus on the things that I loved to do, and I began to do them well.

For the first time, I had trusted and let go of things as I had no choice. I asked for assistance with different areas of our business and these specialists in their areas of business were superstars in my eyes.

They took over the many things that I didn't like to do. I continue to celebrate these experts every day. They only want to use their talents to help us succeed. They are my cheer squad, cheering me on still.

You may be asking how I chose what I didn't want to do. How did I choose what to delegate?

Since I love stationery, post-it notes of many colours became my best friend. At any time of the day, I could write what needed to be done on a sticky note and stick it with the appropriate colour co-ordinated hive I had arrange around the walls of the house.

These were then up for all to see and discuss. It was a great system, as during treatment and even now, some months afterwards, my memory retention is poor at best. I still write things down to this day and probably will always. As I progressed through the notes, I happily took them off the wall. Job done!

Enjoying Life Through Delegation

I'm now just over eighteen months since my cancer diagnosis and my body is doing amazing. It's working on being fabulous once more. Having a diagnosis like this makes you realise how life can change in a second.

It was out of my control and I quicky realised that I still had choices. I had the courage to delegate. I got rid of the stuff that I wasn't that great at because I hated doing them or wasn't quite sure I was doing them correctly.

Now I have time, time to enjoy the smallest of things that I am grateful to be alive to see. My birthday month last year was spent hiding away. Not wanting to be seen.

This year, I'm celebrating being alive! And I'm celebrating month long with the people that mean the most to me. I found a new love for marketing, and I really enjoy it.

I have also realised that everything we do is based on relationships. I value every person I meet. I also love to network. I find it very rewarding to link people with others.

I found a new passion for playing the guitar. I always wanted to learn, but of course I never had time. I'm no Jimi Hendrix, but it's something that clears my mind, like meditation. It helps me be present in the moment and have fun.

I can do this now because I've delegated. I have time. I stay in my superpowers and that's what makes me productive.

Now I have time, I plan my day the night before. I write everything in my diary that I need to do the night before and happily tick off my list as the day progresses. I'm now productive.

I also realise that sometimes things can wait another day because I have a coffee date! This type of planning has also stopped me from lying in bed wasting time at night to run through the things I have to do the next day while I should be snuggled into bed and snoring away.

In doing the best me, I use all my talents and happily do so. I have my cheer squad who I'm accountable to. Not all these people are paid businesses, as I have also teamed up with friends that share the same interests.

One of the biggest achievements this year (apart from being alive) was joining a local women in business network. Do this – it will change your life!

There are other businesswomen with the same issues that you have, and they have tips and tricks that they use to spread themselves throughout their day with work, family and social commitments.

Did I say social commitments? Yes! Be seen and enjoy socialising. We're in our businesses due to the love of them, so share what you do with others when they ask and when you're out socialising. There's no better place to do that than out and about in your community.

If there isn't a women's business network near you, start one today. Don't wait. There are other women out there that need you as much as you need them. They are the beginning of your cheer squad.

Once you've delegated, you will now have the time to socialise, fill your bucket with great juju and power through. You will also be able to give yourself a well-deserved time out. Yes, time out is a great thing. It helps you reset, recharge and maintain yourself at your best.

If I hadn't been forced to delegate, I would still be slamming myself from one task to another and never really finishing anything to the standard I was trying to get to.

I have also just come to the realisation that old habits die hard. They sneak back in when you're not watching to make you flat stick busy again. My husband recently mentioned this from observing me winding my way up to busy again.

I was trying to do so many things that my body still restricts me from doing. I will have a go anyway and then suffer in many ways days later. He reminded me of my promise to always put myself first and always stop when I need to without feeling guilt.

And there, ladies, is my cheerleader. The one who puts up with just enough to let me think I'm boss but keeps me grounded in the process. Your cheerleader can be your best friend, a parent, husband, wife, sister or brother. They are the ones that see you and they get you.

Don't Be Too Busy for Life

When enjoying life, use everything you own. Not just the mismatched plates because you don't want the kids to break the good ones – use the good ones!

Those moments with family and friends are "life's good moments". If you're not prepared to use it or wear it, then sell it. Let someone else enjoy it.

Clutter gets in the way of delegation. It clouds your thoughts and helps with the creation of chaos. And chaos is the outcome of the lack of delegation.

A messy head, due to the lack of delegation creates physical mess, which definitely leads to mental mess. Before you know it, nothing in your life is organised, delegated or on time, and the only solution is to run away to the Daintree and live off grid!

I believed that after being under incredibly high levels of stress and exhaustion for such a long time, I couldn't see any way of changing my habits. I had formed the obsession of doing or trying to do and be everything.

Now, I love the fact that I'm very comfortable that I don't have to do everything or be everywhere for anyone other than myself. Well, maybe myself and my head cheerleader.

It was divine intervention. From wherever or whoever was watching on the side lines, this divine inception had obviously witnessed enough of my madness and made it stop completely in the only way that I would listen, as dramatic and as forceful as possible and without choice.

Conclusion

Celebrate *you* every day. Believe that nothing is impossible, and *you* are the most important human in your world.

There is no other human like you. You are a unique and beautiful human that has a set of skills that, without even knowing, inspire others.

Wear your best shoes out every day. Use the best china your grandmother gave you and always use the silver serving utensils even when you're alone eating ice cream from the tub.

At the end of the day, these items are just things. Love the things you have and enjoy them every day. Smile at a stranger, smiles are free. Have coffee with the people you enjoy being around.

Life is too short to spend time on skills that you don't enjoy doing. If you hate doing your books, there is always an amazing person happy to do them for you!

Do the things you love with the people you love and *stop* trying to be everyone's everything. Remember you are awesome. You are awesome every day!

About the Author

Melanie has lived in the Gympie area for just over 20 years, moving from Sydney with her family. A definite sea change from the hustle of city life to the quietness of rural Queensland.

But Mel isn't suited to quietness. Once moving to QLD, Mel also changed careers from a corporate secretary to school teacher where she has taught in this profession in the Gympie area. Her and her husband, Wayne also began Camelot Camels and Noosa Camel Rides some nine years ago where they share their love of camels where ever they can.

Life changed dramatically for Mel in 2020. Receiving a diagnosis that has changed her life forever. With now a deeper appreciation for life and for the things that are really important.

One of Mel's super powers is her networking skills and building solid relationships with whoever she meets. A strong moral compass and a love of community.

Life means more now and is appreciated every day.

Chapter Sixteen
Recognising Opportunities and Making Conscious, Considered Decisions

By Tracey Browning
Constantine Quilts

Introduction

Some people say that you need to follow your passion to succeed in business. I tend not to believe that. Whether it is running a business as a sole trader or through a company, it does not matter.

What matters is that you are able to identify opportunities that occur while following your passion. If you do that then you can build a successful business by taking advantage of opportunities.

As the eldest child, I worked alongside my dad on our family farm from the moment I could drive at eight years old, and I have since realised just how entrepreneurial my dad actually was!

From experimenting with sunflowers, lucerne and different breeds of sheep, all alongside a small herd of beef cattle. He tried and succeeded in many different areas to pull himself out of a huge debt that occurred when inheriting his small farm.

He consciously sought to educate himself and take risks in his farming choices to better his financial situation. With lots of hard work, frugality and fortitude, he worked his way out of that debt and was able to retire at sixty-two years old.

From 1986 I was in consumer lending in banking at two different banks, starting in the city and then moving to the country and focusing on consumer and rural lending.

I was exposed to entrepreneurs that were unsuccessful and those that were profitable. This opened my eyes to objectively look at the "why". Why were some failing and others succeeding?

For the rural farming customers, their success was 50% dependent on the weather (cropping area), but the other 50% was how they managed their enterprises. I learned so much about running my own businesses from both the city and rural entrepreneurial businesses.

Learning and understanding clarity of purpose and careful consideration of opportunities were paramount to those businesses that were successful.

A Passion Is Born

While there were no quilters in my family when I was growing up, my grandmother was a seamstress and fostered my love of sewing and crafting by teaching me how to sew clothing, knit and crochet.

My first sewing machine arrived for my nineteenth birthday, and I sewed a lot of my own clothes for the next few years.

I started my professional career in a bank and worked in different branches and banks on my way up to consumer lending and securities, as well as corporate banking briefly. I loved the interaction and challenges with consumer lending, dealing with numbers, cashflows and balancing people's expectations on what they could truly afford and achieve.

Once I had moved to my third bank in the city, I discovered a quilting exhibition in rural South Australia (where I was chasing my husband to be) and fell in love with quilts.

Back in the city, I researched and found a comprehensive course in learning the skills to design, draft, hand piece, applique and hand quilt my first sampler quilt – all at TAFE. There were no quilt shops in the city at that time, only a fabric dressmaking shop with a small range of 100% cotton quilting fabrics.

After moving to the farm, getting married and starting a family, I had more time to indulge in my passion of quilting and continued to learn and grow with local mentors. I was never one to follow quilt patterns and started drafting my own – all prior to the internet and owning a computer!

I loved working out the math and writing the instructions. My inspiration mostly came from the various Australian and American quilting magazines that I had subscribed to.

I was encouraged by a friend, who was publishing with the Australian Patchwork and Quilting magazine, to submit one of my designs to be published. This was the start of designing and publishing over sixty-five patterns in magazines, books and newspapers around the world over the ensuing years, including a mystery series in a Canadian rural newspaper where I had the most wonderful emails received from similar farming quilters. It truly is a worldwide passion.

In 1998 I registered my business name "Constantine Quilts" so that I could legally run my first micro business with my publishing and teaching activities. The name originated from our family farm – Constantine Farm – as the original owners came from the town of Constantine in Cornwall, England.

Of course, this name had meaning to myself and my family, but no one else would recognise this until I could regularly use it in all these publications.

This was my first experience in understanding marketing and branding, and I strongly believe that the slow process of providing valuable content with quilt pattern designs was far more beneficial than paid advertising that did not come for many years after.

I published quilt patterns in magazines and had guest contributions in international quilting books from well-known authors that gained me the credibility and name recognition that set me up for success in my retail business that followed.

Sharing My Skills

During this time of making and designing, I started teaching a group of young mums in my house on the farm. They even brought along their young children.

The first lesson was a disaster! Two of the younger boys totally trashed the house. Thereafter, we learned how to keep them amused while their mums learned and sewed their first sampler quilt, with me keeping only a couple of steps ahead with fresh designs for them to learn new techniques.

The process of making a quilt is twofold. The class that lasted ten weeks taught my students how to cut, piece and applique their blocks and how to put them together. The next big step that was not included in this class was putting the top, the batting and the backing together and quilting it all to hold it together.

Half of these students eventually completed their quilts, but I ended up quilting and finishing some for them at a later stage as well – just to get them finished and proudly used.

I loved machine quilting on my domestic machine, but I kept looking and researching the larger industrial machines that were specifically designed to quilt quicker with less stress on your body. These were marketed to those passionate about machine quilting and to create your own home-based business by finishing other people's quilts.

There are many who love creating the beautiful quilt tops but do not enjoy the finishing process, which provided the perfect opportunity for me to expand my business by offering to finish customer's quilts, while paying off my first second hand longarm quilting machine.

Of course, with a big machine I needed both new tools and to learn the art of longarm machine quilting. Machine quilting rulers were primarily manufactured in the US at the time and exchange rates were around one Australian dollar to fifty-one US cents, which made them extraordinarily expensive.

Being a farmer's wife, we discussed this issue and chose to research on creating my own here in Australia.

My "No Frills" rulers by Constantine Quilts were born, along with my first website designed in MS Publisher (oh my goodness, I hear you say!) to sell them nationally and internationally to machine quilters that were flocking to forums and email groups that were popular at the time. Facebook did not yet exist and there were very few companies producing these tools.

With the Australian dollar so low, US quilters started to notice my rulers as extremely affordable, even with international shipping. I started to export them and get noticed online far more than I ever expected or intended.

It was a huge learning curve to understand how to take payments, ship safely and learn to market these.

My biggest opportunity was being invited to teach at a major machine quilting expo in New Hampshire, US, and finding a distributor who could stock my rulers at this show while I was promoting them in the classroom. As a non-resident, I was unable to legally retail these myself.

I eventually ended up with two US distributors for my rulers for a number of years. Before exchange rates and a huge increase in designers and smaller laser cutting machines available resulted in the market becoming quite competitive.

I still design and produce templates here in Australia and recently upgraded them substantially to meet current expectations of the industry. My only competition here are international imports, which are quite expensive.

A New Direction

After I had built my website, I also started sourcing and selling lots of different products that were specifically targeting machine quilters. I grew the retail website to over 1,100 products and upgraded the shopping experience many times over twenty-three years.

My first international teaching experience was in 2005, and since that time I have travelled five times to the US and twice to New Zealand specifically to teach. I have made many trips to attend the International Quilt Market in the US to discover products to bring to the Australian marketplace.

While in the US, I also started researching and learning about all the different brands of longarm quilting machines that were not available in Australia. By this time, I had upgraded from my first brand but still felt that I could find something that was more suitable for me.

Funny story, really! My husband kept mentioning that I didn't need a second machine because I couldn't use them at the same time. But when he and my father-in-law chose to purchase a second harvester for the farm, I stated the same back to them and justified to myself that if they can, then I can!

So, my second longarm arrived right in the middle of harvest, and I had to borrow the ute to drive down to the docks to collect my huge machine, weighing 350 kilograms and spanning four metres long.

I had fallen in love as soon as my new purchase was fully set up. As soon as I shared online the news of my new machine, I had plenty of quilters keen to take a look.

This was the beginning of my role as Australian Dealer for A1 quilting machines. I had met the owner and head dealer of the company at one of the shows that I was teaching at in the US, and they were very keen to get their brand into Australia and find someone who could be both a salesperson and service/support person for their machines.

Twelve months later, I was teaching at the next show in Kansas City, I was researching computerised quilting systems that were being demonstrated and found two potential opportunities for a partnership.

Once I returned home to Australia, I consciously sat down and wrote lists of the pros and cons with my husband. I finally committed to another dealership to sell, install, service and support the Intelliquilter computer system that can be installed on all brands of longarm quilting machines in Australia.

This would have to be the most well considered of all my business ventures and it has certainly paid off. My Intelliquilter was the first in the world off the production line in 2006 and is still used today –simply amazing for a computer that is still fit for purpose after all this time.

Back to that funny story about running two machines at the same time. Well, now I can actually have two machines stitching at the same time with only myself to command them.

The men ended up with two GPS autosteer systems that still need an operator on each and that cost a lot more than the computer systems on my quilting machines. To this day, we continue the banter among us.

Now that I was selling both the longarm machines and computer systems individually and as a package deal, it meant that my retail business was also serving much higher valued customers.

Those that invest over $52,000 in this type of setup to create their own home-based business are serious quilters and determined to make a difference in their own family's lives or simply enjoy their passion to create. A strong component of this part of my business was my support, service and encouragement, which created very loyal customers.

These various components of my business all complement each other and create strong relationships that continue today. These relationships are with retail customers, commercial customers, as well as with distributors and peers.

I always believed that if you prioritise your focus on serving others, then everything else will fall into place.

As a business owner, you have to think as a business owner. You will have to think of how to make your business better, how to make it grow and how to expand it. Each new branch of the business should complement each other and encourage financial growth.

With a lot of effort, Constantine Quilts has expanded and grown over many years of print and face-to-face exposure at shows, and I am proud that my family and I are respected and recognised for those efforts.

My children and husband have contributed by working shows with me, holding strong roles in managing retail sales, communicating with enthusiastic quilters, being technical advisors, being videographers in classes and much more.

All of this was while improving my personal skills as a machine quilter, entering competitions and winning ribbons, gaining experience and sharing valuable information. This gained me credibility and respect within the industry.

The most rewarding of all this was sharing my knowledge and seeing my customers and students excelling with their own work and businesses.

> *"Strive not to be a success, but rather to be of value."*
> **– Albert Einstein**

Education Is My New Passion! For Myself and Others

I have always advocated that my small business customers need to continue to educate themselves to be successful as a home-based machine quilting business. However, in Australia we had limited opportunities to attend classes.

The next opportunity presented itself after teaching internationally at machine quilting shows and seeing the value of providing this service.

The next step of my journey was creating a world class international event called the Australian Machine Quilting Festival (AMQF) and achieving my goal to learn event management skills.

For ten years over five events, I provided international and local educators the opportunity to share their knowledge with machine quilters from across Australia and New Zealand.

I spent time meeting and considering potential teachers each time I travelled to shows in the US and even nurtured new teachers and guided them to learn how to share their skills with others.

I am extremely proud of one in particular who has now pivoted her own business to focus on expanding her teaching repertoire into a full-time occupation. I introduced her to publishing in an Australian quilting magazine where she is now a regular contributor.

Australian quilting magazines are where I started with designing, publishing and gaining exposure for my business, so I am thrilled that I could provide that break for her.

The opportunity to call myself an event manager was a huge personal achievement. I pulled together more than ninety classes for each festival with more than twenty teachers, sponsors, volunteers, and an exhibition hall full of vendors from the quilting and sewing fraternity to showcase all brands of machines and supplies to this growing market.

With no formal training or education from any institution, I learned from my experiences in committees and organisations at a state and national level, on how to plan, research, prepare and execute all the aspects of an event such as the quilting festivals.

As members of this industry, we need to work together to foster growth of our customer base and continue to be successful in our endeavours.

A strong area of personal growth during this period was the opportunity to invest in my own education by joining a mentoring group for two years. The networking along with the heavily focused practical and holistic training on being an entrepreneur and running a business were invaluable to me.

To learn best practises, systemisation, sales, marketing and exit strategies resulted in the opportunity to sell AMQF as a profitable endeavour, and I am thrilled that it will continue to support machine quilters and the sewing industry in Australia.

Many thousands of dollars were invested, but I strongly believe that it has been worth it as it shaped and clarified my future with the direction I am heading now.

Pivoting to Embrace New Opportunities

We know that everything, including quilting, is becoming more accessible online. We are a worldwide community looking for ways to connect, support and learn from each other.

Online tutorials and classes are exploding. All the major quilting magazines have online versions and easily provide access to their back issues. We even have online shopping and much more.

While being a member of my business mentoring group, I attended a conference in the Philippines where one of the presenters was Chris Ducker of Youpreneur. After having a one-on-one discussion, he convinced me that I had some serious skills and knowledge that I was giving away all the time (quilters are sharers) and that I needed to monetise it.

As I am also known as a bit of a tech nerd, though not an expert by any means, this was an area that I was keen to explore. It took some time, and after overcoming some health issues, I finally made the decision to move forward with this concept.

There was lots of research and contemplating the pros and cons before I committed to the idea of providing global access to my advice and training via a membership site with courses.

Initially, to test the idea, I created an evergreen summit purely to provide education on the Intelliquilter software. Anyone can watch for free, with replays for up to twelve hours, so it is available to all owners. However, if they want to watch any replays after the free period, they need to pay a membership fee to do so.

I was thrilled that this has now been running successfully since January 2020 and in hindsight was the perfect time as I had started just before the pandemic spread around the world and online learning exploded.

Next step was to create a space online that delved into far more detail for machine quilters to learn about the business of machine quilting and the maintenance and use of their machines.

I love to see any quilter be successful and enjoy providing just the right tips and skills to enable them to do so. "Machine Quilting Academy" was born to be "the key to your success" for any machine quilter.

To achieve this type of delivery I needed to test, understand and also invest in equipment and software. All of this can get quite expensive, and by nature I am quite frugal and aim to do most things the "farming way" – by myself.

I have learned to research and invest in quality software that I can grow with. Not all have been successful, but enough that have saved me money overall compared with others.

I have discovered that the online world can be really brutal with choices, and I needed to find a safe place to ask my questions and be mentored in this new world of online memberships.

I am pretty happy where I am currently, but I am only just starting and can see so many possibilities to grow and support my members. I am enjoying sharing the different solutions with my membership and training them on how to use them to their own advantage as well.

Conclusion

My journey is ongoing. On reflection, I can see that my underlying experiences early in my career lead me to run my own businesses. Initially, I simply fell into them while pursuing my passion of quilting and sharing my knowledge, contacts and experiences.

Sometimes opportunities just happen, and we run with them because they fall in line naturally with our passions. Other times they can be presented to you, and you may need to actively consider the pros and cons and decide on whether to pursue that opportunity to add to your stable of services and products.

We have a desire to be successful in our business ventures. We want to make a living doing what we love doing. We want to be able to pay our bills and have some left over to enjoy life.

For some, we want to be able to pass on our business and knowledge to the next generation of our family to carry on the legacy. We want to be able to hand over the farm to our children without debt or commitments in supporting us as we retire.

My businesses have been a product of my passions and the desire to be a contributing member of the partnership between my farmer husband and me.

My career is still evolving and hopefully will continue to do so to keep things exciting and challenging while also being lucrative both financially and holistically.

The aim is to stay passionate but also allow the freedom to balance family life – especially with our first grandchild recently born!

About the Author

Tracey Browning has been a passionate quilter and small business owner since 1998. Opportunities kept presenting themselves and the business grew in different directions every couple of years as she found her true path.

From teaching patchwork to locals, to quilting for others, to creating an online retail space, designing and manufacturing then publishing. So many skills were learned and used to build her businesses.

Her online retail space – constantinequilts.com is the largest online supplier of machine quilting products in Australia today after 21 years online.

Selling commercial machines and computer systems took her in the direction of mentoring and supporting quilters across Australia and New Zealand, in creating and succeeding in their own home based businesses, which are ideal for rural and regional locations!

Creating and running an International Festival for 10 years, to provide this niche industry with focused classes with National & International teachers, exhibitors and inspiration was the next step. And now finally, she is creating an online global space to share her years of expertise in both machine quilting, the business of machine quilting and also of her own experiences in publishing, teaching, manufacturing, marketing online and travelling.

Machinequiltingacademy.com is the result. The ultimate aim of this membership is to assist and support machine quilters to be as successful as they want and need to be, to sustain the lifestyle they choose to have.

Chapter Seventeen
Keeping the Businesswoman Alive –
Reinventing Yourself

By Susie Williams
Fleurieu App

What do you want to do when you grow up? Those words are often said to my teenage girls. When I hear it, I cringe, and so do they.

They cringe because they do not know. I cringe because they are kids and why should they know already?

Geez, I just did not know as a kid. Those close to me might tell you that I still do not know what I want to do when I grow up! *Ha-ha* ... maybe not grow up?

I grew up 500 kilometres northwest of Adelaide in South Australia in a regional area called Buckleboo. I have not lived there for over thirty years but still refer to it as "home".

Home was nice and stable, parents and two older brothers, a family held together by hard work on the family cereal and stock farm (well, hard work on my parent's behalf!).

As soon as we arrived home every day on the school bus, we went straight in for some kind of fuel in the form of homemade cooking by Mum, then out the door ASAP to hang with my many pets or being Dad's shadow on the tractor or in the shed or trying to run in my brothers' footsteps and perfect my motocross racing skills for the next weekend.

How on earth did this tomboy end up an entrepreneur? A businesswoman? A wife? A mother?

Bloody hard work, determination (maybe stubbornness is the right word? Thanks, Dad!), a stable family to grow up in, a supportive husband and kids, and the ability to adapt and reinvent myself when needed.

What Is a Businesswoman?

What comes to mind when you are asked what a businesswoman looks like?

Is it the stereotypical woman dressed in a suit and black high heels? Is she often a tad scary and is so ambitious that she gives up the dream of having a family of her own, and is self-centred enough to want success and power more than anything else in the world?

Or is she someone who has always dreamed of her dream job and knew exactly what she wanted and how she was going to get there?

What are the characteristics of a businesswoman? I looked this up to see if it matched my perception.

The top ten characteristics I found are:

1. Self-belief
2. Ambition
3. Confidence
4. Passion
5. Humility and willingness to learn
6. Sense of purpose

7. Assertiveness

8. Hard work

9. Bravery

10. Persistence

Do these pre-requisites remind you of any other role? I am a mother of three daughters, it sounds very much like the job description for being a mother!

The majority of the businesswomen that I have met are the opposite to what the stereotypical description of a businesswoman is. A businesswoman is all the traits above – we use them every day in our work life, just as the businessmen do, but often we are mothers, wives, sisters and daughters.

We coordinate the school calendar, sport calendar, and family social and events calendar. We are the older parents' care and support, and often the backbone of our partners' successful careers. We are the football coach, the support for our brothers, sisters and friends – we are all of that *and* we are the businesswomen.

The businesswoman is the woman that goes to her place of employment, completes her role every day and returns home to do it all again tomorrow. The businesswoman is the self-employed woman that has special skills and crafts that she can do from home to work around her family duties.

She may have created something special and unique to share with the world. She is the eternal entrepreneur, potentially looking for that next challenge as soon as she masters the current one. Which one are you? Perhaps a mixture of the above.

Then there is me. Writing this chapter has been a great way to look at myself and how I do things, or how I view myself.

I am definitely not the businesswoman in the suit. I am also not the totally confident woman that appears to have it all together.

I am the mixture of the above description, the hard worker and the determined woman who wants to make a positive impact on her region through her work.

I want to be the best role model that I can possibly be, I want to make my family proud, and I am incredibly proud to call myself a businesswoman, because until recently that was not actually how I perceived myself.

How Do We Keep the Businesswoman Alive?

For me, one of the key components to keeping the businesswoman alive, even with all our daily expectations and pressure, is about having a close eye on your "why".

What is your personal why?

We all have a why, you just may not have thought about it. Why are you a businesswoman? Does it suit your personality? Did it just happen?

Most of us have made it happen through hard work and promotion, or through adjusting our work situation to adapt to our current family situation.

What is your business why?

To be a businesswoman or an entrepreneur, we chase our business why. What are you trying to achieve? What difference are you making? Is it all about financial gain?

Do Your Personal and Business Whys Match? (Energy and Work Satisfaction)

I believe that the key to keeping the businesswoman alive is that your personal and business whys should align. They are not the same, but you must be able to maintain both aims in life. If pushing hard to fulfil your business why destroys your personal why ... then why would you do it? (*ha ha*, see what I did there!).

You have gained nothing in life if reaching your businesswoman goals destroys your personal goals. This is the hardest part in our working life – finding that work-life balance.

Often, we do not get it right. In fact, anyone that has started a business knows that there are many times that the balance is simply not there. However, if you manage to implement plans along the way – the next long weekend with the family, the next weekend you have planned with your girlfriends – it will help you step away and achieve more balance.

If you ensure that you place an emphasis on the self-love and well-being for yourself along the way – while keeping an eye on your business goals – you will find personal and business success. It sure is a tough balancing act though!

Second Key to Keeping The Businesswoman Alive – Resilience!

Everyone in business needs to be resilient. Actually, each one of us needs to be resilient – you only have to look at the world in 2020/21!

If you are a businesswoman, an entrepreneur and own a business, resilience is key. Why? Let us have a brief look at some of the obstacles in your way.

If you are a wife and mother as well as a businesswoman, "mummy guilt" is a pretty tough one to overcome. I guess you never do totally overcome this one, but you do get better at dealing with it.

What do I mean?

Any mother that has gone back to work after having a child knows exactly what I mean. It is when you head into work and must leave your child behind that is sick, or you stay at home from work to look after your child, then you are feeling guilty that you are not at work.

Yep, it is pretty hard to win.

For some reason, men heading into work do not seem to carry this same guilt. It must be bred into us women. It sure is a man's world!

Usually, there are more men the higher up the ladder you look in a business. According to the Australian Bureau of Statistics, in 2019-2020, managers are almost twice as likely to be men (61.4%) than women (38.6%), and these men often do not have the same understanding of juggling family life and work.

I have also spent most of my working life in a career that is dominated by males. It is lucky that I have a thick skin. Yet, it does worry me, even in today's world, how some women cope in male-dominated worlds, particularly after having children.

It makes me more determined to be a good role model for our girls and help create strong, resilient women.

Resilience and Reinventing Yourself – How Do We Get There?

Permission to screw up. This is crucial for life let alone being a businesswoman! This is how we learn. If you cannot make mistakes and move on, you will destroy yourself.

Keep an open mind. Be open to change. If you are not open minded, you might just miss that amazing opportunity. You might miss that crucial crossroads in your business and indeed your personal life too.

This is how I have managed to add a wide range of expertise to my suitcase, and how I managed to keep my finger in all the pies. This is my unintentional reinvention, and it makes life really quite fun and definitely interesting!

Have patience. This is something I struggle with. We work so hard for what we are doing that we often forget to breathe and be patient. If your business is moving forward, you are doing amazing.

As women, we tend to juggle so much and wear so many hats. This means that we cannot do everything all the time. Be kind to yourself, there is always tomorrow (*geez, I hope I read this and pay attention*).

As important as patience is celebration! **Celebrate the small things**, do not wait until you reach the high goal you have. Celebrate the first client. Celebrate the first small milestone.

Share this with your team and family, you are all in the journey together. Celebrating the small stuff will remind you that what you are doing is amazing and why you are doing it.

Nurture yourself. If you are a mum, you know that no one else will do this for you! As a mother and a businesswoman, if you are suffering and not looking after yourself, your work and family will suffer.

At the age of forty, breast cancer gave me a serious kick up the bum and a reminder that you only get one go at this gig called life. Take the time to eat well, get enough sleep and keep fit.

If you do all three things you are a fabulous role model for those around you, but you will also be more efficient at work. Let alone feel great too.

Grow your support network. This is something until recently in my business life I have not had, nor seen the importance of. I am the type of person that is most comfortable in the background, getting things done but prefer not to be seen. This means that my support network in a business sense has been lacking.

Maybe because I am also stubborn and like to do everything myself?

My current work juggling act has taught me that I need support. Support from my family and friends is luckily a given for me – that bit is my strong point.

Recently, I have realised the importance of building a network of other like-minded people – yes, other businesswomen around me.

I have never sat in a room learning about something and feeling totally comfortable with the company I sit among. I have found a group of women that are all businesswomen in different types of industries, but as a collective group there is no judging, there is only sharing and nurturing of each other and our businesses.

I believe this is the massive strength of businesswomen. We are good at nurturing others.

It is at these networking events that I have realised that I and many other women that start small business seriously suffer from imposter syndrome, the feeling of not being competent enough or not really being a businesswoman.

Finally, another recent addition to my support crew is a mentor.

Very recently, I was lucky enough to have found someone with many more years of experience in the business world than me. Someone I can confidentially chat about my business, someone who is willing to be brutally honest when I need it, and someone who has my back.

This is the most valuable, most recent part of my businesswoman life.

My Story

How Did I End Up Here?

Unless I was going to take on the family farm or marry a farmer, I needed to live in Adelaide and find a job as soon as leaving school. I took a job during Christmas, and this helped me find full-time work fairly soon after school.

I was lucky enough to snag a job in a well-respected, large agricultural research organisation.

As I said at the beginning, I had no real idea what I wanted to do. If I had the opportunity for some outside work where I did not have to wear fancy clothes and make up and I could make a difference to agricultural industry, I was happy.

Here started my lifelong career in agriculture research.

I will warn you that at this early stage in my story, I liked new challenges. I am not sure that I seek them out, but I have always been willing to be open minded and grab change by both horns, rather than cower away from it.

My time in agriculture research spanned over seventeen years within three government research organisations and five different departments. Entomology, Crop Protection, assisting teaching Agricultural Science and Winemaking, sustainable agriculture mapping and Precision Viticulture – all related to agricultural research.

There were always new challenges and different roles.

Growing up on a cereal and sheep farm has no doubt fuelled my desire to continue to improve farming practices. I love working with farmers and growers and keeping my hand in all things agriculture.

Where Did the Businesswoman Come From?

In 2007, we moved to regional New South Wales for my hubby's work. I was working in viticultural research in Adelaide, but my employer would not support me working remotely. I was disappointed, but what can you do?

I was fortunate that I had a great relationship with one of the private companies that we did much of our research and trials with. They had a lot of respect for my capabilities in the GIS (Geographical Information Systems) field that I specialised in and suggested that I work with them as a contractor from my new remote location.

I cannot begin to tell you how excited I was by this opportunity, and with a young family, I was determined to make this work. This was my turning point to taking any changes and opportunities head on, no matter the location.

To this day, I still provide consulting services to the same company that presented the opportunity for me to work remotely and around my family, something I will be forever grateful for. This opportunity also taught me that I can do things differently and work for myself.

Since the change in career from working in and for agricultural research organisations to consulting for the agricultural industry, we have lived in five different regional areas across Australia and New Zealand.

Each move has presented different opportunities for my hubby and I both personally and professionally.

It is not something I would choose to do (moving with a young family is darn hard work emotionally and physically!), but looking back I would never have done anything different.

The lifelong friends we have in each location are the best friends anyone could ask for. The opportunity these moves created for me to reinvent myself – priceless.

We all go through tough times professionally and personally. My tough personal years came around my fortieth birthday. Being a milestone birthday, I decided to tick off a few tasks relating to my health and getting older.

One of these was to check in for a mammogram – just because I could. To my surprise, my results came back positive for breast cancer.

Between selling our house and one of our work-related moves, we went through testing and surgery and soon realised that I had created my own luck, and as my surgeon said I had "dodged a bullet".

By being proactive regarding my health I had successfully found breast cancer in its earliest stages. I had surgery to remove the cancerous area but had avoided further treatment and ultimately saved my life.

We got off lightly, but with three young kids (one a baby still), the experience took its toll. It knocked the wind out of my hubby and my sails for a good year. Just as we started settle down in our new environment and with my breast cancer journey, we were asked to head to New Zealand for work!

While living in Marlborough, New Zealand, my viticulture consulting work slowed down due to tough times for the industry. I was also in another personal low patch having buried my dad a few weeks before leaving Australia.

I went into survival mode for some months, doing the minimum amount of vineyard consulting but trying to keep it together for my hubby's new role and our three young girls' new environment.

To get my businesswoman mojo back, I threw myself into one of my hobbies – photography.

I studied remotely and grabbed work where I could. The desire to learn more about a new skill was infectious. The more I learnt about the camera and taking different kinds of shots, the more I wanted to improve and learn.

I reached out to the owner of a local magazine and asked if I could become part of the team. I started by taking the odd shot for the business advertising material until I found myself the main photographer for the magazine. I was then invited to take photos for feature stories and nestled my way into the team.

In my true form of reinventing myself, enjoying challenges and wanting to make a difference, I proposed an idea to the magazine.

My hubby and I have moved a lot, and everywhere we moved, we threw ourselves into exploring our new surrounds, making the most of the time we were there. We would chat with our new local friends about our discoveries as newcomers, and to our astonishment, often they had never explored the places we had.

To me this was unbelievable. Why do people not explore their own backyards?

I proposed the idea of doing a monthly feature where I would explore something relatively local, take photos and write about the experience, with the idea of encouraging the locals to explore their own backyards.

It was incredibly popular for our readers, and some of the experiences I created for myself and our family were just breathtaking.

My other desire is to help make a difference, in people's lives and especially with other small businesses. This has always burnt inside me, and I believe this is due to having grown up where I did.

As a child growing up in a remote country town, I was exposed to seeing the effect of what happens when people do not shop local. If you do not spend money on the local businesses, they eventually close. Each time that happens, the community shrinks.

It can be totally devastating for regional towns.

Hence, upon our return to Australia, the Fleurieu App was born, designed to put everything for the Fleurieu Peninsula and Kangaroo Island at your fingertips.

The focus of the app is to keep communities alive with their local news and sport provided by local journalists, and to provide a place for local businesses to be listed and advertise so we can support them. The Fleurieu App is a platform for the local community, businesses and the visitors to our region.

It is no "walk in the park" career, but I feel intensely satisfied with my reinventions and learnings along the way.

I satisfy my desire to help the agricultural sector to keep on moving in a sustainable way, working with farmers and keeping myself tied to my roots.

I get to help small businesses in my local community and support the community, while reminding each one of them about the most amazing part of the world we live in.

I am present and flexible for my hubby and children (not always, but as much as I can), and as we all know, our kids are not home for long in the big picture.

Yep, keeping the businesswoman alive is bloody hard work, but it helps pull my big picture together.

I would say that I have created a work-life balance ... almost.

I still have plenty of working years ahead of me and I am so excited to see what other opportunities I get to create and how I can reinvent myself into the future years.

Life is short, we need to make the most of it.

My parting words to you, my new friend – *you've got this!*

About the Author

Susie Williams is the owner and director of the Fleurieu App and a Precision Viticulture GIS (geographical information systems) consultant. She grew up at Buckleboo, a remote part of the Eyre Peninsula in South Australia. Her farming upbringing is the backbone of her passion for rural communities. Both her viticultural consulting and creation of the Fleurieu App are testament to her desire to help rural business and communities.

Regularly moving, thanks to her Husband's work, has provided the platform for Susie to continually reinvent herself and her career. Determined to make the most of every regional location they have lived, has created opportunities for Susie to adapt and thrive both personally and professionally.

Surviving breast cancer at the age of 40 has helped this already determined woman live life to the fullest with her family and has helped mould the resilient businesswoman she has become.

Susie has a bachelor's degree in Natural Resource Management and a Certificate in Digital Photography.

She enjoys down time in nature, hiking and camping with her family and friends. She gets inspired while competing with her fellow dragon boat team members and learning to surf with other inspiring businesswomen.

www.fleurieunews.com.au

www.fleurieuapp.com

www.susiewilliams.co.nz

https://www.linkedin.com/in/susie-williams-243171102/

Conclusion

I hope that you feel inspired, motivated, more confident and more trusting after reading the stories from these amazing rural businesswomen.

Building a business from the bush isn't always easy. Some of you are facing those very first steps into business, while others are a little further along. Regardless of where you currently stand on the business journey, growth is always possible. Getting to where you want to be can always be done.

Now, let's conclude with a bit of a recap.

In the Mindset section, we heard from Janiece about believing in yourself and your business to achieve big things. Jo gave us a crucial run-down on balancing masculine and feminine energy in business.

Clare gave us insight into how we can find our tribe in rural locations. Steph gave us the psychological skills we need to thrive in adversity, and Linda shared her incredibly heartfelt story around overcoming obstacles.

The Getting Started section provided us with Anna's ideas on how you can bootstrap your business in the early days, just as she did.

Gillian gave us the inspiration to forever embrace learning. Lisa encouraged us to find those all-important gaps in our market. And finally, Sarah gave us a practical step-by-step guide to starting a business from scratch.

In the Marketing section, I'm sure you'll agree that Jenn's chapter on Making Marketing a Priority was potentially business-changing *and* life-changing. Pip gave us insights from her experience in marketing her start-up.

And yes, there were two chapters from me on copywriting and digital marketing essentials. I sincerely hope you found this section useful.

Finally, we had the Systems for Growth section. Emily's comprehensive chapter on bookkeeping is vital to keep close at hand. Business finances and record keeping need to be managed carefully and correctly if you want to succeed.

Recognising opportunities, courtesy of Tracey, reminded us that opportunities can be found everywhere if we remain open to them and learn to spot them.

Susie reinforced the message that as businesswomen, we are forever evolving as we go through both life and business. And Mel's story of sudden health challenges demonstrated that we should not try to be "superwomen" who do absolutely everything – delegation is important for our own wellbeing and those around us *and* we will end up growing our business faster and more easily.

Phew! There's a lot there, right?

Yet, it's important that you don't let it overwhelm you. There is great advice in this book, so simply pick and choose the steps you need to tackle for where you're at, one at a time.

Further Assistance and Information

If you're looking for more details on any of the amazing contributing authors in this book, or simply looking for your next best step forward, the journey with us doesn't have to stop here.

Visit www.ruralbusinesswomen.com.au where you can continue your learning, download extra resources and find out more about our authors.

Take Action

Finally, it's time to go out there and build the business of your dreams.

No matter where you are across rural, regional and remote Australia – anything you want can be achieved.

You've seen the proof through the eyes of the authors in this book.

Nothing happens without action. The trick is to just get started. One teeny, tiny step at a time.

Or do what I do and just throw yourself off that metaphorical business cliff – trusting that the parachute will be there when you need it!

Sarah Walkerden

www.ingramcontent.com/pod-product-compliance
Lightning Source LLC
Chambersburg PA
CBHW071600080526
44588CB00010B/965